CONTROLLING THE BOTTOM LINE

CONTROLLING THE BOTTOM LINE

(A guide for businesses who are more concerned with increasing profits than sales)

William E. Perry

An Inc./Van Nostrand Reinhold Publication

VAN NOSTRAND REINHOLD COMPANY
NEW YORK CINCINNATI TORONTO LONDON MELBOURNE

82566

Manufactured in the United States of America

Published by Van Nostrand Reinhold Company Inc.
135 West 50th Street, New York, N.Y. 10020

Van Nostrand Reinhold
480 Latrobe Street
Melbourne, Victoria 3000, Australia

Van Nostrand Reinhold Company Limited
Molly Millars Lane
Wokingham, Berkshire, England

Macmillan of Canada
Division of Gage Publishing Limited
164 Commander Boulevard
Agincourt, Ontario M1S 3C7, Canada

15 14 13 12 11 10 9 8 7 6 5 4 3 2 1

Library of Congress Cataloging in Publication Data

Perry, William E.
  Controlling the bottom line.

  "An Inc./Van Nostrand Reinhold publication."
  Includes index.
  1. Industrial management.   2. Managerial accounting.
I. Title.
HD38.P439 1984   658.4'013   83-21814
ISBN 0-442-27380-0

To GOD, who provided the original and best control guidelines—the Ten Commandments. If we all lived according to these commandments, most other controls could be eliminated.

preface

The giants of American industry in the early 1900s had little trouble controlling the bottom line. The story has been told of many of the founders of major U.S. corporations that they went into their accounting office at year end and said, "I want X percent or X dollars profit." The accountants then reworked the financial statements to produce the desired profit.

Entrepreneurs today have more difficulty in dictating the amount of profit that appears on the bottom line. Although accounting gives some leeway in controlling the amount of profit, the rules are much more stringent than they were fifty years ago. However, today's entrepreneurs still have many avenues open to them for controlling the profit on the bottom line.

Controlling the Bottom Line is a book about making money. Controls are one of the great misunderstood aids to profitability. The book suggests that controls are not for accountants but rather are the friend of management; in fact, they make things happen. It is through controls that honest people remain honest, workers provide a fair day's work for a fair day's pay, and management acquires the proper information to make effective decisions.

The objective of this book is to demystify how and what to control in the business. The suggestions are based on the experiences of many organizations. The concepts work. My thanks go to the businesses that have taught me these concepts and to the losses the businesses incurred before learning how to build effective controls.

William E. Perry

contents

CONTROLLING THE
BOTTOM LINE

I
Are controls worth the effort?

There are two ways to make money: one is to increase sales and the other is to reduce costs. Controls help do both.

1

there is more than one way to make money!

To control or not to control—that is the question. Or perhaps the question is: should I control, and if so, what? There may be more misconceptions and misinformation about control than any other single topic in business.

Let's explore a few of the myths about control:

1. *The primary purpose of control is to stop people from stealing.* Of course, controls want to stop people from stealing, but the primary purpose is to stop losses of all kinds. Stealing, while substantial, may not be the largest loss.

2. *Controls cost money.* Not only are controls free; they may be the single greatest generator of profit in the organization. If controls don't provide a positive return on investment, they should not be installed.

3. *Controls slow down progress.* Wrong! Bad controls may slow down progress, but well-designed and effective controls permit tasks to be performed better and more quickly. For example, visualize trying to go from one side of your city to the other during rush hour without traffic lights.

The objective of this chapter is to encourage you to like controls. That's right—like controls. Perhaps you never thought you would like controls, but for a few moments forget your biases and attempt to judge controls on their merits. If at the end of this chapter you still don't like controls, give the book to a business in financial trouble . . . . they are probably suffering from a lack of controls and may be ready to take the control cure.

THE TWO BEST MONEY-MAKING SCHEMES

Everybody is looking for a quick way to make $1 million. Magazines are filled with ads offering a book explaining the success formula for millionaires for the everyday low price of $9.95. Each author promises to divulge *the* method that not only carried him or her from rags to riches but can do it for you too.

Get ready now for one of the first benefits of this book. I'm going to save you the $9.95 by telling you right off what the success formula is. In fact, better than that, I'm going to divulge to you the two best ways to make a million dollars, which are:

Number one way to make $1 million

Increase your current annual sales to a level that will produce $1 million in profit.

Number two way to make $1 million

Decrease the cost of your sales to a level that will eventually permit you to make $1 million on your current rate of sales.

If you don't feel that bit of information will help you become a millionaire, you share the feelings of many who bought a get rich quick book. Using controls is not a get rich quick concept. Controls are a way of life that will help maximize your profits.

The information in the success formula is absolutely correct. The method to increase sales or reduce costs is all that is needed to start you down the yellow brick road. The missing ingredient is how to do it.

Controls are designed to ensure that business transactions are processed in accordance with the intent of management. If management designs good marketing strategies and procedures and if those are followed in accordance with management's intent, sales should increase. If management has designed good policies and procedures for performing work, then costs should be minimized. Let's look at some examples of how control might have helped improve the bottom line.

Some Lack-of-Control Examples

Three real-life examples of how the lack of control decreased profitability follow. Each case will be explained and then the control aspects of that case will be discussed:

Case 1—The "One for You, One for Me" Caper Many small businesses receive cash as payment for items they sell. Employees greet the customer, find out what the customer wants, deliver the desired product, then price and collect the money from the customer. As employees learn this system, they frequently add a new wrinkle. When they collect the money from the customer, some of it goes into their pockets and some into the company's pocket. The methods are many. Some employees put the money and the sales slip aside to pocket later; others wait until slack hours when they are working alone; and others simply palm the money.

Control Problem Most skimming occurs when there are weak controls over the recording of sales or collection of cash. The "one for you, one for me" caper exists most frequently when the sale does not have to be recorded in a controlled manner at the time of the sale. In this case each dollar lost came directly from the bottom line.

Case 2—The Idle Money Mess This corporation was relatively prosperous. Sales were going well, and money was flowing into the bank. With the need to invoice customers, answer inquiries, and prepare tax forms, there was little time to reconcile bank statements or move monies between accounts. Therefore the bank accounts were reconciled when time was available, and money moved at the same time. On top of that, the company had a super credit rating because bills were paid as received.

Control Problem This company was suffering from a chronic case of money mismanagement. Funds were lost due to keeping large balances in noninterest-bearing accounts and paying vendors before the due date. In some instances money was lost because the company failed to followup quickly on customer checks returned due to nonsufficient funds. What may have seemed like a control burden cost the company several thousand dollars in the course of the year—again, all bottom-line profit.

Case 3—The Poor Adder Problem A medium-sized merchandiser hired numerous sales clerks. The clerks were required to identify the product sold, record it on a sales slip along with a price, calculate the sales tax, and develop a total for charging the customer. Unfortunately, the clerks made a lot of arithmetic mistakes. When overcharged, many customers complained, and the invoices were corrected. When under-charged, many customers overlooked the error and walked away with a bargain.

Control Problem   The business assumed that the school system had done its job in teaching the clerks math skills. However, a good system of control assumes very little. If anything, it assumes that bad things will happen and works either to detect them or prevent them from occurring. The company could have installed a multitude of controls to reduce this threat. Such controls would include using prehiring tests to determine the clerks had mastered arithmetic; providing them with adding machines or even pocket calculators; and giving them tables showing sales tax and other product extensions.

The stories go on and on. However, each has the following central themes:

1. The cause of the loss is common—and usually known.
2. The loss could have been prevented or reduced by a control.
3. The monies saved through control flow directly to the bottom-line profitability of the organization.

A LESSON IN CONTROL ACCOUNTING

Accountants have been counting the beans of business for hundreds of years using the following accounting formula:

Income from sales	$XXX.XX
Less cost of sales	XX.XX
Gross profit	$ XX.XX
Less administrative expenses	XX.XX
Net profit	$ X.XX

This accounting equation, like our two success formulas for making a million dollars, explains what has happened but not how it has happened. The business person looking at the financial statements knows whether or not the company is making money, but may not really know why. Also, if the amount of net profit isn't satisfactory, the manager may not know precisely how to improve it.

The problem with many small accounting systems is that they don't contain the proper chart of accounts. The chart of accounts determines how many buckets the beans fall into. For example, if we don't have an account for damaged inventory, we will never know how much inventory was damaged.

Control accounting is a term I have devised to indicate an accounting system with a control orientation. In other words, it identifies what needs to be controlled and then begins to develop some accounts to control those areas. Some of the financial accounts that can be used for control purposes include:

- Bad debts
- Damaged inventory
- Computation errors
- Mispriced products
- Losses due to fraud and embezzlement
- Inventory sold at less than normal price
- Inventory scrapped

The financial statement that could be prepared if this type of information were collected would tell a story of control problems. The underlying message is that you can't control what you can't see. This message tells one of the underlying problems in the concept of control. It's a strange paradox which is:

> *An item is not controlled because management believes it's not large. At the same time, the magnitude of the loss is not known because it is not controlled.*

The Rule of Thumb in Control

Control is more of an art than a science. There is no one way to control, just as there is no one way to close a sale. On the other hand, there are many good control principles, just as there are many good marketing principles.

The principles I believe are effective in improving a business's profitability have been reduced to thirty-two rules of thumb. These rules may not appear in the textbooks on control theory, but down in the trenches where the money changes hands, they work. You may want to skim through these rules of thumb (see Appendix A) before you read the book to gain a layperson's look at how controls really work. The first control rule of thumb follows:

CONTROL RULE OF THUMB 1
You can't manage what you can't control.

WHAT ARE CONTROLS?

Once upon a time a small business person enjoyed the fruits of a good business location. To his dismay, he learned that a large department store was opening next to his business. To make matters worse, a few weeks later another large department store announced plans to open on his other side. He pictured the two huge department stores with his own small store nestled in between and thought, "I am doomed." The small business person thought and thought about the type of control that could prevent his profits from eroding when the huge department stores opened. At last the idea came to him. On the day the two stores had their grand opening with their banners flying, he would post a huge sign above his store that stated "MAIN ENTRANCE." The sign worked, it drew customers into his store.

Control should be designed to help reduce losses. The small businessman in the preceding story used a control to point out where his store was located. Too often we are blinded by a narrow definition of control and fail to realize the true meaning of control.

A *control* is anything that will reduce the probability of a threat turning into a loss. Examples of controls include a lock on a door to prevent unauthorized entry, a physical count of inventory to determine if any is missing, one clerk checking on another to make sure an arithmetic computation is performed correctly; and a corporation buying keyman life insurance on a difficult-to-replace executive. Controls are the totality of procedures, methods, tools, and techniques directed at reducing losses.

Controls are broad in scope but have the following three criteria associated with them:

1. *Threat.* A threat is any unfavorable condition of concern to the business. Examples include fire, theft, inventory spoilage, and statutory sanction.
2. *Loss.* There must be a probability of the threat becoming a loss. Equally important is the potential magnitude of the loss. For example, the loss due to spoilage of fruits and vegetables in a supermarket is potentially much greater than the loss of someone stealing the empty bottles returned for deposit.
3. *Control.* There must be some method, procedure, tool, or technique that will reduce either the probability of loss or the magnitude of the loss.

To have a control without a threat is a waste of money. To have a significant threat without a control is foolish. It's not a chicken-and-egg situation. In the control/threat scenario the threat comes before the control. Control begins with a threat, and continues as long as the threat persists.

Threats to businesses can be divided into six general categories. These are the categories of threats that if not controlled can turn into business losses. It is the objective of controls to reduce these threats so that the losses due to those threats are insignificant in size. (See Figure 1-1.)

The six major threats to a business are:

1. *Mismanagement*—failure by the business managers to instigate those policies and procedures necessary for running the business or to provide adequate direction for the business.
2. *Theft and fraud*—assets of the organization will be taken by employees and outside parties. Note that while robbery is a threat within this category, nonviolent crimes will account for most of the losses.
3. *Statutory sanctions*—fines and penalties levied on the organization for failure to comply with a local, state, or federal regulation.
4. *Abuse*—the damage or destruction of assets due to willful or careless acts by employees and nonemployees.

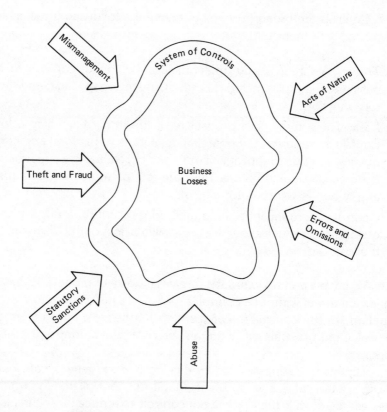

Figure 1-1   BUSINESS THREATS

5. *Errors and omissions*—the improper performance of duties by employees.
6. *Acts of nature*—destruction caused by events not under the control of people, such as flooding, fire, and wind damage.

   Of the six categories of threats, most losses will occur due to either mismanagement or errors and omissions. However, losses due to theft and fraud can be extensive if the controls of the business are weak. While these three categories may represent the major portion of losses for most businesses, management should evaluate all six categories to ensure the business is adequately protected against losses.

AREN'T CONTROLS FOR ACCOUNTANTS?

Management of any business has four basic responsibilities: organizing, planning, directing, and controlling. For some reason the control responsibility seems to be delegated to the accountants.

A study of the business school curriculums discloses an absence of control courses. To my knowledge there is no business school that teaches a course devoted exclusively to control. There are also very few books written on the subject of control. You might conclude from this that the subject is of no interest or is boring. On the other hand, you might conclude that people do not really know how to control business systems.

Control may be the world's second oldest profession. Its roots date back, say, to 2,387,162 B.C. when Lioness Leader had a management problem with her tribe. Lioness instigated the control that when anyone objected to her rule she would hit them over the head with a club. Lioness found that this control was effective in assuring that events occurred in accordance with the intent of the tribal leader—in other words, people did what Lioness said.

Since that time most controls have been oriented at hitting people over the head in one way or another. Since senior management tires of this role quickly, they like to delegate that responsibility to the controller of the club. The position has evolved into one in which the controller of the business is generally believed to have the responsibility for control.

Unfortunately, management still retains control responsibilities. To convince the nonbelievers, in 1977 the Congress of the United States passed the Foreign Corrupt Practices Act. This Act covered all corporations covered under the Securities and Exchange Act of 1934. The law made it both a criminal and civil offense if management did not devise and implement a system of internal controls that was adequate to ensure that transactions were processed in accordance with the intents of management.

People tend to concentrate their efforts in areas where they feel comfortable. Unfortunately, many managers do not feel comfortable in the area of control. A person's comfort level can be increased by two acts. First, he or she can study an area to learn more about it. One of the objectives of this book is to provide that basic knowledge. Second, the individual can practice what he or she has learned. The control rules of thumb provided in this book are designed to help in establishing good control practices.

CONTROL RULE OF THUMB 2

When you want to know who is responsible for control, look in a mirror.

HOW GOOD ARE THE CONTROLS IN MY BUSINESS?

One of the first control questions that management must ponder is: How good are my controls today? Obviously, if your system of controls is good, there is no need to spend a lot of time studying and improving them. Your time may be better spent on other areas of the business. On the other hand, if your control dike is leaking cash, time expended in plugging those holes may do more to increase profitability than trying to shake a few orders loose from your customers.

Controls are like marriage. You are either married or you are not; you either have a control or you do not. If a control is not in place, working and effective 100 percent of the time, it is not the type of control you can count on. For example, would you buy fire insurance if it were good during the working hours of your business but not effective during nonworking hours?

Questionnaire 1—"How Good are My Controls?"—is designed to provide you with a preliminary assessment of the adequacy of your controls and to give you an initial indication of the amount of time you should be devoting to them. It's like taking temperature: the higher your temperature, the greater the concern you should have for your health. Stop reading and take a few minutes to answer the ten items on the questionnaire on page 13.

Assessing How You Stand on Controls

The questions in Questionnaire 1 are meant to be predictors rather than a comprehensive assessment. For example, you could go to a doctor and the doctor might note that you are overweight, underexercised and

Questionnaire 1   HOW GOOD ARE MY CONTROLS?

Number	Item	Yes	No	Comments
1	Is someone in your business responsible for the adequacy of the system of internal controls?			
2	Has your business identified the types of threats that could cause losses?			
3	Have controls been established for each of the significant threats?			
4	Do you know your cash-flow position for the next six months?			
5	If your business were to lose 5 percent of your monthly revenue through theft or errors, would your accounting system detect that loss that month?			
6	Do you know the percentage of profit that you are making on each of your products, or at least all of the major products?			
7	Have you performed background checks on the integrity of your employees?			
8	Does your business develop marketing and financial plans and then plot its progress against those plans?			
9	Do you periodically check to determine that the controls you have established are in place and working?			
10	Are all cash receipts and payments controlled by either prenumbered documents or automatic recording devices such as cash registers?			

that you have high blood pressure, and excessive vices such as smoking. Based on these predictors, the doctor might state that you are a candidate for a heart attack. This does not mean that you will have one but rather it is probable that someone in your condition will have one.

Questionnaire 1 is designed so that *yes* answers are indicative of good control practices, and *no* answers of poor control practices. Just because you have poor control does not mean that you are necessarily experiencing losses due to the inadequacy of those controls. It does mean you have a high probability of having losses. As in the case of the imminent heart attack, in which you might want to change your behavior, so might you want to improve your controls if your control environment is such that losses might occur without detection.

Total the number of *no* answers you checked on Questionnaire 1, and then look for the appropriate following interpretation.

Number of No Answers	Interpretation of Result
0-2	You have a good system of internal controls. Read this book at your leisure. You might pick up a few ideas to help keep your system of control current with your changing business environment.
3-4	You have potential weaknesses in your system of control that should concern you. It would be advisable to do a detailed study of your controls in order to identify potential weaknesses. Read this book as soon as practical and make any necessary adjustments.
5-6	You could have serious control problems. The probability exists that you are already experiencing large losses due to inadequate controls. Don't sleep until you have read this book through. Tomorrow morning begin implementing the control practices described in this book.
7-10	Padlock the front door of your building. If people aren't stealing from you, they should—you have made it easy for them. In businesses of this type, improving controls is usually essential to survival. Don't reopen your business until you have read this book and installed many of the recommended controls.

A ROAD MAP THROUGH THE BOOK

This book is designed to teach you all you ever wanted to know about controls—and probably much more. The book is divided into three parts to answer the following three questions:

Part I: What are controls, what do they do, and how do I implement them?
Part II: What type of controls should I have in my business?
Part III: How do I know my controls work?

An overview of the three parts follows:

Part I: Are Controls Worth the Effort?   Chapter 1 was designed to acquaint you with the objective of control and to provide a self-assessment to determine if an organization has adequate controls. Many businesses are hurt through employee theft or abuse. Chapter 2 attempts to answer the question of whether the business is being ripped off. Finally, Chapter 3, the meat of Part I, describes the strategies management can use in building an adequate system of controls.

How to Use Part I   This part is for senior management to assist them in establishing control strategies. The material is designed to be read once and then put into practice.

Part II: What Needs Controlling?   Controls have been defined as the means for reducing threats. However, threats are general and controls are very specific. For example, there is the threat of fraud and theft, but controls to reduce that threat must be installed somewhere in the business. This part divides the business into the following areas for control purposes:

- Chapter 4, Controlling Revenue-Generating Activities, deals with sales, cash receipts, and movement of product or services.
- Chapter 5, Controlling Credit, Receivables, and Collections, covers determining who should get credit and how much, the recording of receivables, and collection policies.

- Chapter 6, Controlling the Purchasing-and-Payables Activity, discusses purchasing, the receipt of goods, and payments.
- Chapter 7, Controlling Inventory, covers accounting for inventory, physical inventories, obsolescence, and loss of inventory.
- Chapter 8, Controlling Cash, deals with bank accounts, cash flow, and investments.
- Chapter 9, Controlling Payroll and Personnel Activities, discusses personnel policies, salary administration, integrity, morale, and day-to-day employee activities.
- Chapter 10, Controlling Profitability, addresses planning, budgeting, pricing policies, and monitoring against plans.
- Chapter 11, Controlling Record Keeping, covers establishing a proper set of books, statutory sanctions, tax reporting, and monitoring the record keeper.

How to Use Part II   Part II should be helpful to both senior management and line management in understanding the detailed threats and controls faced by their business. However, the material is designed primarily as a reference manual for line management to use in designing a system of control for a particular area, such as inventory. Periodically, managers should review the material and adjust the controls accordingly.

Part III: Do the Controls Work?   This part is designed to help evaluate the effectiveness of the system of controls. It provides the necessary tools to conduct an audit of the system of controls. Control assessment in many organizations is delegated to the internal auditors. If the corporation cannot afford to staff an internal auditor function, management can fulfill that role using the material in this part of the book. Chapter 12 provides a work program on how to determine if the controls work. Chapter 13 covers monitoring and adjusting controls so that they can be neither abused by management, nor allowed to become obsolete.

How to Use Part III   The adequacy of controls should be assessed periodically, at a minimum, annually. This part of the manual provides the work program and the necessary explanatory material to conduct that review assessment. Each time the assessment is conducted, this part of the manual should be reread and the appropriate work program implemented.

CONTROL RULE OF THUMB 3
Controls don't earn money—but they can increase profits.

2

are you being ripped off?

The United States Chamber of Commerce states that white-collar crime is a $40-billion-a-year business in the United States and growing. It ranks as one of the major industries within the United States; since the take is almost pure profit, it may be *the* most profitable industry. The odds are that your business is contributing to this lucrative trade.

Statistics by numerous law enforcement agencies indicate that over 90 percent of the business losses due to fraud and embezzlement are committed by employees. The range of employee criminals runs from the lowest-level clerk to the president of the organization. Unfortunately, our greatest enemy is the employees of our own organizations.

This chapter covers the scope of the business crime problem. First the responsibility for crime is identified and the enemy described. The chapter describes the eight most common methods used to steal from organizations and provides a simple self-assessment to help you determine the probability that ripoffs are occurring. The chapter ends with twelve tests you can use to determine if your business is being ripped off.

WHO IS THE BUSINESS CRIME CULPRIT?

There are two common themes in business crime:

1. The individual with the greatest opportunity usually commits the crime.

2. The crime normally occurs at the point where the controls are the weakest.

Using these characteristics, one can almost predict who will commit a crime and at what point the crime will occur. In fact, many law enforcement agencies use exactly these two assumptions to detect business crimes. The *penetration-point technique* attempts to identify the one individual with the greatest opportunity to commit a crime and the point within the business where controls are the weakest.

If we are able to predict with reasonable accuracy who will commit the crime and where the crime will occur, then who is the culprit? In my opinion, senior management of the business is the culprit. Let's look for a minute at what senior management might do to prevent themselves from being ripped off:

1. *Reduce the temptation to commit a crime.* If the business makes it too easy for a person to steal, then the person will steal. One company has adopted a policy of assessing the amount of temptation offered to an individual after a crime has occurred. If the company has made it too easy for the person to commit a crime, then management believes it is a contributor and does not prosecute. On the other hand, if the individual has not been overly tempted, then the organization believes it is not a contributor and so prosecutes the individual.
2. *Reduce the opportunity to commit a crime.* We assume from books and movies that sophisticated means are used to commit crimes, but in actual practice criminals use very elementary methods. For example, why is it necessary to do anything complicated if one can take money directly out of the cash drawer without detection? Each time the controls are strengthened, the opportunity to commit a crime decreases.

Management should never be surprised when a crime occurs. What should surprise management is that it had an opportunity to strengthen the controls which it probably did not take. Business crime is an ever-present threat and requires the constant attention of management.

The responsibility for the prevention and detection of business crime rests squarely on the shoulders of management. Normally, crime occurs not due to bad luck but because management did not recognize its responsibility and take the appropriate steps necessary to prevent or detect the criminal act. Let's ask ourselves a couple of questions about business crime.

Who is the Criminal?

The profile of the individual who commits white-collar crime against his or her organization reveals that such a person:

- Has above-average education and skills
- Is well-liked
- Holds a position of trust within the business
- Performs above average on the job
- Works harder than most other employees
- Generally gets to work earlier and stays later than most other employees
- Knows the systems of the business well and frequently suggests means for improvement

If I ran a business, this is exactly the type person I would want to hire and keep. All of the traits that appear to be desirable in an employee frequently appear in the individual who commits a crime against a business. Let's look at the types of positions these people hold:

- Responsible for accepting and recording transactions
- Is a first-line supervisor
- Maintains accounting records
- Has senior management responsibility (other than owner)

Another interesting paradox exists in the backgrounds of those who commit business crime. When organizations hire ex-convicts and other people with questionable backgrounds and work records, those individuals rarely commit crimes against the organizations. The reason is simple. Management does not fully trust those employees and thus provides the necessary controls and monitoring to ensure that they do not commit any crimes. Normally, they know they are being well controlled and watched and thus have little incentive to attempt a crime when there is a high probability of detection.

On the other hand, our typical criminal with the impeccable

background and credentials does not appear to need watching. Therefore, he or she is trusted and given jobs in which the conduct of a crime
becomes easy. Unfortunately, many trusted employees bend to the
temptation and defraud their employers.

What Are the Common Ripoff Methods?

Crime is an old profession that has been perfected over thousands of
years. Because of its high profitability, criminals are willing to invest time
and effort in some ingenious but normally simple techniques. As previously stated, criminals look for the easiest method to commit the crime.

Some violent crimes occur in which guns or other weapons are
used. However, these rarely account for large losses and at the same
time invoke the wrath of the law enforcement agencies. It is a far greater
crime to take $5 at gunpoint than to embezzle $1 million from the same
organization. The white-collar criminal who took $1 million will be
embezzling again years before the armed-robbery convict gets out of
prison.

Most business crimes occur through the use of one of the following
eight techniques:

1. Transaction trickery
2. "One person's junk is another's treasure"
3. Shell game
4. Passing the baton
5. "Et tu Brute!"
6. Spoofing
7. Salami
8. Bonnie and Clyde

These techniques are briefly described in Figure 2-1 and explained in more detail below.

1. Transaction Trickery

Description: This is the most popular of all the criminal techniques. The objective is to alter a transaction in a manner that benefits the
individual. Transactions can be added; for example, an invoice can be

Number	Methods	Description
1	Transaction trickery	Transactions are added, deleted, or modified in a business system.
2	One person's junk is another's treasure	Everything has a value. Frequently those items that appear worthless and are not controlled are readily marketable items.
3	Shell game	Record keeping or products are moved around so that the location is not known in order to divert them to the possession of an employee.
4	Passing the baton	An employee and a friend work together to remove products or cash from the organization.
5	"Et tu Brute!"	A trusted employee takes advantage of that trust for personal gain.
6	Spoofing	The business is led to believe that a particular event is true when in fact it is not. The spoofer uses that fact to advantage.
7	Salami	A small amount of money is taken a large number of times.
8	Bonnie and Clyde	A feature of automated technology is used to benefit an individual before the enforcement agencies have learned how to control that technology.

Figure 2-1 BUSINESS CRIME CATEGORIES

inserted into the accounts payable to be paid. A transaction can also be altered; for example, the dollar amount of a sale can be reduced so that the employee can pocket the difference. Or the transaction can be deleted, such as an accounts receivable record from a friend. Because the point of origin of a transaction is frequently one of the weakest points in the system, it is highly susceptible to manipulation.

Example: Jane works in a small dress shop. One day six dresses of the same style arrive. Jane likes the dresses and picks out one for her personal use. The receiving records are changed to show that only five dresses arrived. The invoice for six is paid without noting the difference.

Prevention: Appropriate segregation of functions so that at least two people are involved in all transactions. This eliminates most problems. One person should conduct the transaction and a second either record or check the transaction. For example, one person could order a product and another receive and store that product. In addition a third person could compare the order to the receiving document to determine that what was ordered was received.

2. One person's junk is another's treasure

Description: Scavengers make a living picking items out of the trash and then selling them. Many charitable groups collect old newspapers and aluminum cans as a means of raising money. Employees often look for apparently worthless items for the purpose of confiscating them and selling them to third parties.

Example: The wife of a corporate officer notices a company truck driving through the residential areas on a regular basis. The truck is carrying wooden pallets used in the warehouse. The pallets are expensed when acquired or built and are not inventoried on the book. When an investigation is undertaken, it is found that an employee is stealing the wooden pallets and selling them in the black market. Surprisingly enough, there is a thriving black market in wooden pallets.

Prevention: Items can be controlled without being carried on the financial records of the corporation. A simple count as to the number of pallets being acquired and scrapped would give a running inventory that could be counted periodically. Sometimes all that is needed is to give the appearance of control, and the desirability of taking the product diminishes significantly.

3. Shell Game

Description: The normal commodity for theft is a product. This poses a problem in getting the product from under the nose of management into the sole possession of an employee. In the original carnival shell game a hustler moves a pea from under one shell to another and then to a third by quickly switching and lifting the shells. The object of the game is to guess under which shell lies the pea when the hustler stops. The "customer" always misses because the pea has actually been removed. Likewise, employees that are fast enough can shift the location of products until successfully removed from the premises.

Example: Department stores are prime candidates for the shell game. Both employees and customers shove merchandise into bags, purses, and pockets. Clothing is taken to the dressing rooms and then worn under the individual's old garments as a means of getting the product out of the store.

Prevention: A variety of controls are used to reduce the shell-game technique. Spotters can look for people slipping merchandise into their garments or bags. Clip-on devices can trigger an alarm when objects are removed from the store. Employees can be searched as they leave the premises to catch thieves.

4. Passing the Baton

Description: This technique involves the collusion of two or more individuals. It is one of the harder techniques to prevent because it normally involves play acting. The technique can involve two employees, or an employee and a customer of the organization. Together they work to remove products or funds from the organization.

Example: Supermarkets are hurt by this technique. Friends of a cashier go through that cashier's line and remove many more items from the store than they pay for. The clerk either rings up a lesser amount, or, when there are sensors, moves it through the sensor without triggering the reading device.

Prevention: Many supermarkets have a policy that a clerk cannot ring the groceries of a friend. If the policy is well known, then with appropriate threats such as immediate dismissal, an employee will be very reluctant. While the manager may not know a friend is going through the checkout line, other cashiers may, and if they are good employees will note the exception to the manager.

5. "Et tu Brute!"

Description: Employees put into positions of trust frequently abuse that trust. Many times the crime begins with a few dollars; then the person takes a few more to cover the first few. While many of these employees honestly believe they will repay the amount taken, it frequently grows to such a large amount that repayment is really not possible.

Example: An accountant in a trucking organization has the responsibility of paying the bills. One is the Mastercard account. The accountant has been given his own company card for taking people to lunch and for filling up the company car with gas. However, the accountant used the charge card to take friends to dinner, buy personal merchandise, and so forth. When the bills come in, the accountant charges his personal expenses to the inventory account and then pays them. When the embezzlement is detected, the business has lost over $25,000.

Prevention: Division of responsibilities works. No one should be put into a position where they can both perform an act and conceal the same act. If two or more people are involved, what one does, another checks.

6. Spoofing

Description: Spoofing is a method by which one person tricks another into believing a particular event happened which did not. The spoofer then capitalizes on that event to the detriment of either the individual spoofed or the business. There are many variations of this technique. It is one of the oldest and yet still more effective techniques for ripping off an organization.

Example: On a Friday night an individual dresses up in a guard uniform complete with badge, billy club, and pistol. The individual handcuffs a money pouch to his wrist and goes to a local bank night depository station after the bank has closed. The individual places a sign on the night depository that says, "The night depository is out of order—please leave your deposit with the bank guard." As depositors drive up weary from a long day's business, they drop their day's earnings into the pouch handcuffed to the bank guard. After a couple of hours the individual walks away with several thousand dollars in cash.

Prevention: An educated customer and employee base is the best detriment to spoofing. Employees particularly should be requested to report immediately any unusual circumstance. If the spoofing scams are known, employees and customers should be made aware of them.

7. Salami

Description: The salami technique is a method of taking a few pennies from a lot of people in order to gain a little spending money. If you have ever been in a delicatessen and watched the counter person take out a roll of salami, cut off a slice, and then put it back, you know that it's not possible to tell that a slice has been cut from the roll. The same is true in this kind of embezzlement. A few pennies or even a fraction of a penny is taken from numerous accounts, which over time add up. This technique works best with computers.

Example: A small business of 500 employees has a computerized payroll system. At year end the payroll programmer deducts $1 from the federal withholding tax of each employee and added the $500 to his own federal withholding tax. All of the books balance, and the employee gets an extra $500 refund from the Internal Revenue Service.

Prevention: Businesses should be very suspicious when an employee or customer reports their account to be off by a couple of pennies. The first reaction is, "So what!" However, with the salami technique in mind, it is advisable to determine what happened to those two cents before dismissing the discrepancy.

8. Bonnie and Clyde

Description: Criminals have always taken advantage of new technology long before businesses learn how to control that technology. Each new technological advance in business has associated with it abuse of that technology. This occurs because control traditionally lags behind technology. It is not until the problems become known that controls are developed. This window between the distribution of technology and control of technology is a high vulnerability period for businesses.

Example: Bonnie and Clyde were notorious bank robbers in the early 1900s. The technology they exploited was the automobile. Bonnie and Clyde would rob the bank and then run out to their automobile, driving off into the sunset while the law enforcement agencies attempted to chase them on horseback. It wasn't until police started using automobiles that Bonnie and Clyde were put out of the bank-robbing business.

Prevention: Businesses acquiring new technology must contemplate how that technology can be abused. Playing "what if" may disclose some of the methods that might be used by criminals to utilize new technology for their own advantage. Once the technological threat is known, controls can be established to reduce that threat.

WHAT IS THE PROBABILITY MY BUSINESS WILL BE RIPPED OFF?

The following two conditions normally have to occur before business crime occurs:

1. A vulnerability must exist in the system of controls.
2. An individual must want to defraud the business.

When both of these conditions occur, there is a high probability that a crime will occur. On the other hand, a business could have large vulnerabilities with no one taking advantage of them.

In determining whether your business will be ripped off, you are playing a game of probabilities. We can do much better identifying the existence of a vulnerability than we can identifying a perpetrator. However, you need to recognize that if individuals are led to the watering trough too often they eventually will sample from the trough.

A ten-question business theft self-assessment questionnaire is included as Questionnaire 2. It is designed to be answered by a member of senior management. The questionnaire lists ten criteria. Each question should be answered to indicate whether the criterion is very applicable, applicable, or not applicable to the business. The assessment is as follows:

• *Very applicable.* The criterion is on target and fully describes the way the business is run.

Questionnaire 2 SUSCEPTIBILITY TO BUSINESS CRIME

Number	Criteria	Very Applicable	Applicable	Not Applicable	Comments
1	Management tends to overlook small employee abuses, such as being late to work, borrowing a quarter from the cash register for coffee, or taking a few supplies home.				
2	Many key elements of the business are under the complete control of trusted employees of the business.				
3	The controls over cash receipts are generally weak. Controls do not exist that provide a proof that all sales were recorded and all cash received and deposited.				
4	No audit or review is conducted to evaluate the adequacy of controls or the correctness of employees' work.				
5	There is basically no division of responsibilities in the organization. Tasks are completely assigned to single individuals to perform.				
6	Once employees are trained, there is little supervision and monitoring over the work they perform unless the employee raises a problem for supervision resolution.				
7	The controls over inventory are weak. Generally there are no controls that can reconcile the change in inventory to the recorded sales of the business.				
8	The prevention of employee theft is not an important part of the business. Generally management never discusses their policies regarding employee theft.				

Questionnaire 2 SUSCEPTIBILITY TO BUSINESS CRIME

Number	Criteria	Very Applicable	Applicable	Not Applicable	Comments
9	Generally the controls over purchasing and receiving of products are weak. There is no reconciliation between what is ordered, what is received, and what is paid for.				
10	The accounting system does not record and report variances from expected norms, such as inventory shortages, bad debts, or product returns.				
	Totals				
	Very applicable × 3 = _____ Applicable × 2 = _____ Not applicable × 1 = _____ Susceptibility score = _____				

- *Applicable.* The criterion is sometimes applicable and sometimes not.
- *Not applicable.* The criterion does not fairly describe the way the business performs its work.

Carefully examine each of the ten criteria and then determine the applicability to the business. Stop reading at this point and answer Questionnaire 2.

Evaluating Susceptibility to Business Crime

Total the number of checks in each of the three columns in Questionnaire 2. Then multiply the number of "very applicable" checks by 3, the number of "applicable" checks by 2, and the number of "not applicable" checks by 1. These three numbers when added will give you a susceptibility score, which can be interpreted as follows:

Susceptibility Score	*Meaning of Score*
10-15	Your susceptibility to business crime is very low. If it does exist, it will probably not be in large amounts, will be detected very quickly after it occurs, or both.
16-20	Your business is a candidate for employee crime, but you have the opportunity of detecting that crime within a reasonable period after it occurs. Your business could probably reduce your business crime vulnerabilities significantly at very low cost.
21-25	Your business is highly susceptible to business crime. While you may catch or prevent some types of business crime, you are vulnerable to others. You should conduct an investigation to determine if crime has occurred. In addition, you need to tighten your system of internal controls.
26-30	Your business has one or more business crimes just waiting to occur. As soon as someone wants to rip you off, he or she will. You should undertake two events immediately. First, tighten your system of controls significantly as soon as possible. Second, conduct those tests necessary to determine if you have already been hit by a business crime.

CONTROL RULE OF THUMB 4

A good system of internal control keeps honest
people honest.

HOW CAN I TELL IF I HAVE BEEN RIPPED OFF? (OR, THE TWELVE GOOD RIPOFF TESTS)

When a criminal walks into a business and sticks a gun in the owner's nose, there is no question that a crime is occurring. On the other hand, when an employee silently sticks his or her hand into a cash drawer and removes money, the announcement that a crime has occurred is missing. However, telltale signs of the crime exist in either case and can generally be detected in either case.

The methods of detecting a nonviolent crime are significantly different from those used for detecting a violent crime. In a nonviolent crime there are no alarms blaring, no broken windows or jarred doors, no gagged and tied employees, or other evidence of brutality. However, to the trained eye the trail can be just as clear. Just as the search dog can sniff out dope, so can the trained investigator sniff out business crime. Fortunately, many of the techniques are easy to use.

Twelve of the better business crime detection methods are listed in Figure 2-2 and individually described below. Figure 2-2 indicates briefly the objective for using each of the techniques. Note that it would be unusual for any organization to use the entire dozen methods, but it may choose to use more than one.

Popcorn Test

Movie theaters are concerned that people will get into the theater without paying. It would be easy for friends of the ticket taker to enter the theater. Ticket takers are usually low-paid employees, and turnover is quite high. Therefore, while it is difficult to prevent this type of thing from occurring, it is not that difficult to detect its occurrence. Movie theaters keep good records on the amount of popcorn sold. They know that there is a direct relationship between the number of people entering the theater and the number of boxes of popcorn sold. If popcorn sales indicate that more people entered the theater than tickets were sold, management is alerted to the fact that there is a high probability of people entering the theater without paying. Once this is known, investigation can be undertaken to confirm and stop the condition if it is occurring. Most businesses have these type of relationships. What is needed is to look for the relationship and then use it to detect potential business crime.

Number	Name of Test	Purpose of Test
1	Popcorn	To use relationship testing to identify problems.
2	Vacation	To spot potential embezzlers, who are never sick or away from work for any purpose.
3	Perform and conceal	To determine if any individual can both perform an event and conceal it.
4	Gross profit	To identify inventory shortages.
5	Sniff	To search out events that appear abnormal.
6	End of the spectrum	To spot potential suspects among employees that appear to do too much or are disgruntled.
7	"Oh, by the way"	To investigate clues from friends, employees, or customers.
8	Surprise	To review periodically an employee's work on an unannounced basis.
9	Consistency	To look for unusual variance in the same item in two different accounting periods.
10	Customer turnover	To determine if someone is stealing customers.
11	Trend	To look for changes in a revenue or expense account that appears abnormal.
12	Rotate	To move people to different jobs so that someone can evaluate the areas where another person has been working.

Figure 2-2   RIPOFF DETECTION TESTS

Vacation Test

An employee that takes no vacation would appear extremely desirable. Employers should be thrilled to death that an individual wants to stay and work, rather than go play for two or three weeks. However, experience has shown that many of these hard-working trustful employees have an embezzlement going and are afraid to leave for fear of detection. Management should keep records on the days employees are away from their work station. If over an extended period of time an employee is never gone for sickness or vacation, management should become suspicious and review that employee's work on a surprise basis. It is important to note that the better controlled major corporations require their employees to utilize their vacation. Those employees in positions of high trust are asked to take at least two consecutive weeks at a time.

Perform-and-Conceal Test

This is a test used by many auditors. If they do a preliminary survey of a company, they look for employees who can both perform an event and conceal the fact that the event has been performed. Some typical examples of perform and conceal are:

- Writing checks and then reconciling the bank statements
- Posting the accounting records and then closing the accounts and preparing the financial statements
- Ordering merchandise and approving payment for the merchandise
- Buying a product and then paying for the product

Whenever an employee can both perform an event and conceal it, he or she has a great opportunity to defraud the organization. For an example, an employee who has the two jobs of writing checks and reconciling the bank statements could write checks to him or herself and post it under a legitimate account. No one would ever see the payees's names or know that the bank balance shows higher than it actually is.

Gross-Profit Test

This is a test used by accountants to identify inventory problems. To perform the test, two conditions must occur:

1. Sales must be reported by product.
2. Inventory records must be maintained by product.

When these conditions occur, the gross-profit test can be utilized. The inventory used in an accounting period is determined by taking the old balance, adding receipts to it, and subtracting the closing balance. The inventory consumed is then multiplied by the average selling price per item of inventory. The resulting amount is compared to the actual sales. If they are approximately the same, it is assumed that all inventory has been accounted for. However, should there be a variance between the calculated gross profit and sales, the difference should be investigated. Obviously, one cause is that someone is either stealing inventory or sales receipts. Another reason for the variance might be that the wrong product was shipped to the customer. In that case, some other product should be shown as having too little inventory removed during the accounting period.

Sniff Test

Over a period of time, managers get to know their business. When events are not going the way they traditionally do, things seem to "smell" bad. Some of this bad odor might be caused by:

- One customer hanging around too often.
- An employee who appears to be spending more money than he or she is making.
- An employee or customer acting funny.
- Some item found to be stored in the wrong location.

Managers should use their intuition to smell out potential problems. When things look wrong, they probably are wrong. It's generally advantageous to investigate, normally after hours, to determine if something unusual is happening.

End-of-the-Spectrum Test

The spectrum in this test is employee attitudes. If at one end of the spectrum an employee is too willing to do everything, that should be equally as suspicious as an apparently disgruntled employee. Obviously, we are much happier with the hard-working dutiful employee, but someone who is taking too much authority, coming to work too early and staying too late may be ripping you off just as much as the disgruntled employee who wants to get even with you because you are making money.

"Oh, by the Way" Test

In the course of a business day a lot of information is transmitted to managers from friends, employees, and customers. These people frequently "smell" problems and because of it bring events to the attention of a manager. Since this third party is not accusing anyone of wrongdoing, it is sort of an off-the-cuff type of comment. However, many business crimes are detected through this method, so these clues should be immediately investigated.

Surprise Test

There is nothing like a surprise to catch an employee unaware. If someone is doing wrong and you investigate their work at an unannounced time, there is a good probability that you will uncover the problem. However, managers should be cautioned in using this type of investigation. If it is a normal part of the business, employees will find it acceptable. If it's abnormal, employees may feel that they are not being trusted, which can have a very negative effect on employee performance. Many large organizations use this technique to conduct surprise cash counts, inventory counts, and so on. Employees should be told in advance that such practices will be used. Note that the warning itself is a deterrent to business crime.

Consistency Test

Month-by-month or year-by-year comparisons between the items listed on the income and expense statement and on the balance sheet can pinpoint potential problems. For example, if a particular financial account is off significantly—for example, if the charges made to bad debts have grown significantly in one month or one quarter—this might indicate that the account is being abused. If requested, accountants can easily provide this type of item-by-item comparison. Also, the financial statements can show the percentage increase or decrease from the previous month, previous year, or whatever period is applicable for comparison.

Customer-Turnover Test

The loss of customers may be one of the more serious losses a business can suffer. Many businesses try to get promises from their marketing and sales people not to take customers with them if they leave. Unfortunately, this is rarely enforceable by law. On the other hand, knowing when customers are potentially lost provides the business an opportunity to attempt to get them back. If it is possible through the business records to determine any significant losses in customers, that loss should be investigated.

Trend Test

Trends tell changes over extended periods of time. This is frequently helpful in detecting wrongdoing. For example, if inventory shrinkage or other vulnerable accounts are increasing, it might indicate that that account is being used to cover up business crime. The consistency test is normally used on the financial accounts, while trend tests are used on items that do not appear on the financial statements.

Rotate Test

Rotation means moving employees from job to job or from one group of accounts to another. For example, a clerk who normally processes accounts receivables for customers whose firm names begin with the letters A–N might periodically shift with the accounts receivable clerk handling customers in the N–Z category. The objective of doing this is for one employee to determine if any hanky-panky is being carried on by the other employee.

HOW CAN I STOP BUSINESS CRIME?

Real estate agents will tell you that in selling a home there are only three important criteria involved in the sale. These are location, location, and location. In reducing business crime, there are likewise only three important methods to consider. These are internal control, internal control, and internal control. The single most important method for reducing computer crime is internal control. Surprised? Many people are. However, the same techniques that are effective in reducing mismanagement, errors and omissions, statutory sanctions, and abuse are also effective against reducing business crime.

CONTROL RULE OF THUMB 5

The way that you spell relief from business crime is
I-N-T-E-R-N-A-L   C-O-N-T-R-O-L.

3

control strategies

The failure rate for small businesses is very high. Only three out of ten remain in business more than one year. The most frequently cited causes for failure are poor financial planning, inexperienced management, and inadequate accounting. To a great extent, the sense of frustration and the threat of failure caused by these managerial and accounting deficiencies can be alleviated by implementing an effective system of internal control.

Most smaller businesses have limited experience in control design. Many feel that control is the province of accountants and auditors and that their business cannot afford this luxury. Many falsely assume that it is cheaper to incur small losses than to pay the high cost of controls.

This chapter provides guidance in understanding and implementing controls in the small business. The control strategies of the small business are discussed, and low-cost, effective ones are suggested. A step-by-step process is described for building controls. The chapter concludes with a plan of action for senior management to use in building a low-cost, effective system of controls for its business.

WHAT ARE MY CONTROL CHOICES?

Controls come in three basic flavors (see Figure 3-1). You can select any or all of the three categories to prevent threat. The choices available are:

- *Event controls.* These are controls that are designed to reduce threats at the point where the threat occurs. Accountants frequently call this the *economic event.* It is anything that either creates or consumes resources. For example, events would be making a sale, shipping mer-

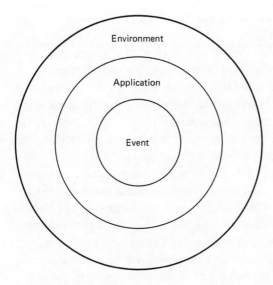

Figure 3-1   LAYERS OF CONTROL

chandise, giving the customer change, paying an employee, and so forth.

- *Application controls.* These controls cover the totality of economic events within a single area of the business. The most common applications are sales, cash receipts, payroll, purchasing, inventory, and cash management.
- *Environmental controls.* These controls govern the way the entire business functions. The controls cross two or more application areas. Frequently, these are called general, managerial, or administrative controls because the development of the control is the prerogative of senior business management. Areas of environmental control include personnel policies, working conditions, customer relations, and business security.

These three categories of control can be viewed as layers of control protecting the resources of the organization. Since the generation and expenditure of resources are centered around economic events, all three categories of control are designed to protect either groups of or single events. In larger businesses the layers of control can be divided among different people or departments. In smaller businesses this may not be practical.

It is not uncommon in smaller businesses for the event controls and application controls to be governed by the same individual. For example, the person making the sales has responsibility for the accuracy of the sale and may also have responsibility for performing the application control of reconciling sales to cash receipts. While it may be desirable to divide the controls among several people, it may not be practical or cost-effective, depending on the size of the business.

Small businesses tend to rely much more heavily on environmental controls than do larger businesses. Environmental controls are centered heavily around personnel policies, and accounting-type controls such as the ripoff tests described in Chapter 2. For example, management may not be able to build good application or event controls over people entering a movie theater but can instigate an environmental "popcorn" test to evaluate the reliability of the processing of events.

Chapter 1 described six general threats facing a business, which are mismanagement, theft and fraud, statutory sanctions, abuse, errors and omissions, and acts of nature. It was emphasized that controls should be designed to reduce each of these threats. We now need to determine which of our three control choices—controlling the event, controlling the application, or controlling the environment—is most effective against which threat.

The recommended control choice strategy for reducing threats is illustrated in Figure 3-2. For threats that economic events will contain errors or omissions, controls should be directed at the event. At the point where an event occurs, controls should be installed to ensure the

Control Choice	Threat Addressed
EVENT (transaction)	Errors and omissions
APPLICATION (such as payroll)	Statutory sanctions Theft and fraud Abuse
ENVIRONMENT (total business)	Acts of nature Mismanagement

Figure 3-2 REDUCING THREATS

accurate, complete, and timely recording of the event. If errors and omissions are caught at a later point, it may be of little value to the business other than knowing the type of mistakes that are occurring. For example, if the cash box is short at the end of the day, there may be no way to recover those funds from the customers.

Application controls are effective at reducing the threats of statutory sanctions, theft and fraud, and abuse. Most statutory sanctions are directed at the incorrect or untimely submission of tax forms. These can be addressed by controls that provide correct application information, such as total payroll dollars and schedules for completing and filing tax returns. Theft and fraud usually occur at the time an event occurs. Since the person controlling the event is frequently the one committing the theft, there may be little that can be done to stop it at that point. However, application controls should be able to detect that a loss of resources has occurred, which can start an investigation and either recover or stop the problem. Abuse is a general threat relating to people not performing their job properly or taking advantage of the business. For example, employees may indicate they need to work overtime when they really don't or may drive the company car for pleasure. Application controls should be able to detect variances from the norm and thus detect abuse.

Environmental controls are most effective at addressing acts of nature and mismanagement threats. Applications can do very little to control fire, wind damage, and so on. Through environmental controls, management can install sprinkler systems, buy insurance to offset losses, and so forth. Mismanagement involves poor business decisions by management. Because these decisions normally affect several applications, they need to be addressed by such managerial controls as planning and budgeting.

HOW MUCH CONTROL IS ENOUGH?

Controls are rarely designed to, nor should they be expected to, reduce threat to zero. Controls can be compared with the collision policy on an automobile with a deductible clause. The reason people subscribe to a $50 deduction, say, is that it is cheaper to pay the $50 loss than to pay the significantly increased insurance premium. In fact, it may cost more than the additional $50 a year to have the insurance company pay the entire loss than if the policyholder pays the first $50 personally.

The level of control established in any threat situation can be considered a control dial (see Figure 3-3). The dial is set by management. At the starting point of the dial losses may be very high because there are no controls. At the other end of the dial there are no losses because controls have in effect reduced to zero any losses due to the threat. One of these dials is set for each threat, like the threat of theft of merchandise.

Management sets the dial to an acceptable level of loss. In the automobile collision example, we set the dial to a $50 loss. In Figure 3-3 we can now visualize the arrow pointing to $50. If we had set the dial to no loss, our insurance premium or cost of controls would have risen. If we had set the dial to $100 loss, the amount of premium would have been reduced from the $50 level. If we had decided not to set the control dial, then it would be sitting on the maximum loss, which in the case of our automobile could be a loss up to the value of the automobile.

Most controls work under the 90/10 rule. This means that 90 percent of the benefit of controls can be achieved for 10 percent of the cost of the maximum controls. Most effective controls are very economical if the dial is not set too high. For example, if we want to eliminate every probability of employee theft, the cost may be very high. On the other hand, some fairly effective controls, such as subjecting employees to searches as they leave the premises, providing warning signs that management will prosecute every instance of theft regardless of amount, and alerting supervision to their responsibility to detect employee theft

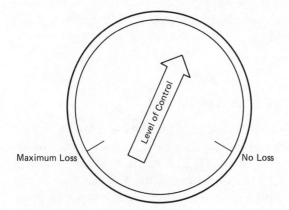

Figure 3-3   CONTROL DIAL

are all examples of low-cost controls that have proved very effective in reducing employee threat.

MANAGEMENT CONTROL STRATEGIES

Control doesn't just happen; it must be planned, implemented, directed, and controlled. Yes, control must be controlled just like any other aspect of the business. If controls are not controlled, they get out of control and may in fact inhibit work effectiveness.

Control must be planned. Developing control strategies is the key to control planning. The strategies represent management's approach to the establishment of a system of controls.

Five major control strategies are recommended as follows:

- *Emphasize people.* People are both the cause and the solution to control concerns.
- *Prosecute violators.* Management actions state whether or not it really believes in its system of controls.
- *Optimize cost-effectiveness (of controls).* As a general rule, you should never spend more for controls than the benefits received from having those controls.
- *Assign accountability.* People do those jobs better for which they know they are personally accountable.
- *Overcontrol sensitive areas.* If the credibility and integrity of part of your business is essential to the survival of the business, install whatever controls are necessary to ensure survival.

The five control strategies, listed in Figure 3-4 with a brief explanation of purpose, are described in detail below.

Control Strategy 1 — Emphasize People

There are two basic strategies for control. One is to control people and the other is to control transactions. Most larger organizations develop elaborate controls over transactions. These controls include division of responsibilities, logs, automated processing controls, approvals and authorizations, and so forth.

Number	Control Strategy	Purpose
1	Emphasize people	People are the key to control
2	Prosecute violators	If you give an inch, you'll lose a mile
3	Optimize cost-effectiveness	Use control dollars wisely
4	Assign accountability	Groups don't protect assets
5	Overcontrol sensitive areas	Survival

Figure 3-4 RECOMMENDED CONTROL STRATEGIES

By the size and nature of their business, most smaller corporations rarely have the time or staff to install elaborate transaction controls and so must rely on their people for adequate control. People-oriented controls include accountability, self-checking devices, and ripoff-type tests. Accountants use the term *compensating controls* to mean that where it is not possible to have effective controls over the processing of the economic event, and in some instances the application itself, then compensating controls can be installed to offset the lack of the primary control. In many instances, the missing primary controls are transaction oriented.

Emphasizing people does not mean trusting people in the sense that they are considered beyond reproach. It means maximizing the skills and talents of the people to do the job right the first time, giving them the appropriate controls to self-check their own work, and then to use compensating controls such as the popcorn test to assess the correctness of processing.

Control Strategy 2 — Prosecute Violators

Management either believes in control or doesn't believe in control. If you tell your children to be in the house at 9 o'clock at night and they come in at 9:01, they have violated the control. But you say, "It's only one minute." Suppose they come in at 9:02, then it's only two minutes; if they come in at 10:00, it's only sixty minutes. If 10:00 o'clock is bad, is 9:59 bad? Using this type of logic, we install a control and then use situation ethics to interpret the control every time a violation occurs. This is an unacceptable control strategy.

If people steal, they should be prosecuted. If people knowingly violate control procedures, they should be reprimanded. If people consistently violate control procedures, they should be fired.

There are two important facts of life that require a management control strategy for prosecuting control violators:

- *Fact of life 1.* People will probe to find the real control policy. Ask your children to come in at nine and they will test you by coming in at 9:05. If you say nothing, they will come in at 9:10 the next time until they eventually find the point that is unacceptable to you. Through practice, your employees will redefine your control policy if you're not strict in enforcement.

- *Fact of life 2.* Small violations encourage large violations. Employees who can get away with small violations may be tempted for a variety of reasons to commit larger ones. For example, an employee who is able to get away with borrowing small amounts of funds from the cash drawer for lunch or other emergencies may be tempted to borrow larger amounts when the emergencies become larger. This fact of life not only results in losses for the business but may unfairly tempt employees to commit crimes when they otherwise would not.

CONTROL RULE OF THUMB 6
Most large embezzlements begin as petty theft that is allowed to continue without reprimand.

Control Strategy 3 — Optimize Cost-Effectiveness

The economics of control are well known, normally practiced, but rarely formalized. We know that it is not economical to utilize a very expensive control to prevent a small loss. For example, we would not hire a full-time guard to prevent employees from taking pencils and Scotch tape home. On the other hand, we recognize that potentially large losses must be controlled. For example, if we knew we couldn't recover from loss due to fire, we would acquire the necessary controls, such as a sprinkling system, fire alarms, fire extinguishers, and fire insurance. We know that the cost of these controls is considerably less than the potential benefit they bring to our business.

The recommended management control strategy is to evaluate the cost-effectiveness of preventing each threat. The concept is illustrated in Figure 3-5, which shows that as the loss due to threats is reduced the cost of controls increases. An important control principle is that the loss associated with a threat is the total of the dollars lost due to the threat plus the dollars expended for control. For example, if customers steal $1,000 worth of merchandise from a store a month and the store spends $500 a month to prevent customers from stealing merchandise, the total loss associated with the threat of merchandise being stolen is $1,500 (that is, the $1,000 loss of merchandise plus the $500 of controls). Looking at the lefthand side of Figure 3-5, you can see that the loss curve plunges more steeply than the cost curve rises. This illustrates that for each dollar spent on controls the loss is reduced by more than a dollar. At the point where the lines cross, the business is spending $1 in control to reduce $1 of losses. This is the optimum point of control. To the right of this point, where the cost curve rises more steeply than loss curve drops, businesses will be spending more than $1 in controls to reduce losses by $1. In the overcontrolled situation, it would be more economical to the business to accept the loss than to control it.

The cost-effectiveness strategy requires management to accept the

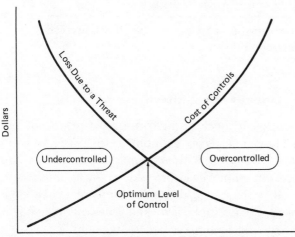

Effectiveness of Control in Reducing Threat

Figure 3-5   COST-EFFECTIVENESS OF CONTROL

concept that in many instances it is cheaper for the business to lose money than to attempt to prevent those losses. Many businesses use their resources ineffectively to reduce threats when it would be cheaper to accept a loss. Examples include situations in which the company is overinsured, pays too many taxes rather than face an audit, or spends more money salvaging scrap than it is worth.

CONTROL RULE OF THUMB 7

In any threat situation, management must determine whether it is more economical to accept losses than to control them.

Control Strategy 4 — Assign Accountability

All sorts of accusations have been hurled at groups and committees. It has been stated most unkindly, for example, that an elephant is a horse built by a committee. The underlying problem with a committee is that no one is responsible. Action evolves from the group.

Committees do many things well, but one thing they do not do well is enforce controls. For example, if five people use the same cash drawer and cash is missing, the finger pointing begins. Each member of the group of five points to the other four, stating that one of them must be responsible.

The recommended control strategy is to identify each item requiring control and then make one individual accountable for control of that item. Using this strategy, the following two things happen:

1. Individuals know that their job, reputation, integrity, and perhaps some of their personal resources may be dependent on how well they fulfill those control responsibilities.
2. If problems occur, management knows exactly where to pinpoint responsibility. There is no multiple finger pointing. The accountable person is responsible.

Listed below are a few of the areas in which individual accountability can be assigned in businesses:

- Management of petty cash fund
- Issuance of inventory
- Purchasing of merchandise
- Management of money
- Maintenance of equipment
- Storage of office supplies

Control Strategy 5 — Overcontrol Sensitive Areas

All areas of a business are not equal. Businesses generally build their reputation on their excellence or expertise in one or two key areas. For example, restaurants may build their reputation on the caliber of their food and service. If either one of these areas should be jeopardized, the restaurant might go out of business. If a food inspector charges a restaurant with violating cleanliness practices in the kitchen and if those violations are made public, this might—and in many cases has—put a restaurant out of business.

These highly sensitive areas warrant more extensive controls than the other control strategies would dictate. For example, to correct health violations in the kitchen of a restaurant may only cost a few hundred dollars, and thus one might argue that it's not worth spending the money to control the cleanliness of the kitchen. On the other hand, the true loss may be the entire business.

This control strategy requires that management first identify the highly sensitive areas of the business and then install whatever controls are necessary to prevent serious problems from occurring in those areas.

DEVELOPING CONTROL SOLUTIONS

The solution to a control concern begins with identifying a threat. Until the threat can be identified, there is no basis or reason for developing a control. If there is a control in your business for which you cannot identify a threat, get rid of that control.

A control solution is a development of a method, process, tool, or technique to reduce a threat. It takes time and effort to build effective controls. If the threat is a concern to you, then it is worth taking the time to build the control well. A poor control may do more harm than good. You don't want to get into the situation of putting in a control, then not enforcing it or changing it because it doesn't work. If the threat is only of minimal concern, maybe you do not even need a control.

Control is a five-step process. It need not be long or time consuming, but they do need to be performed. Designing controls is not an instinct or god-given ability. You must learn how to design controls if you want them to be effective. The process is simple, but it needs to be followed.

The five steps are illustrated in Figure 3-6 and individually described below.

Step 1 — Identify the Threat

The control design process should be a regular part of doing business. The process begins each time a new threat is identified. That threat will be dealt with through the remaining four control solution steps. It is then up to management to ensure that the control retains its effectiveness over time.

Chapter 1 identified six general threats. Chapters 4 through 11 will define specific threats that need to be addressed for each application. By definition, a threat is any condition that could cause the business to lose money. In the first step of the process, define the threat in detail. For ex-

Number	Step	Purpose
1	Identify the threat	To determine what may need controlling
2	Determine if the threat is worth controlling	To decide whether or not to control the threat
3	Select the control solution	To design a method to reduce the threat
4	Select the method to monitor the control	To design a method to measure the effectiveness of the control
5	Implement the control	To make the control work

Figure 3-6 CONTROL DESIGN PROCESS

ample, employee theft is a general threat. For control purposes, the threat must be defined more specifically, such as realizing that an employee could steal money while receiving a customer's cash. General threats are difficult to deal with, whereas specific threats can be controlled.

Step 2 — Determine if the Threat Is Worth Controlling

It is important to identify as many threats as possible. However, each threat does not require controls. Control is implemented in accordance with the control strategies discussed earlier in this chapter.

The two questions that managers must ask themselves about each threat are:

1. How much is my business likely to lose because of this threat?
2. Can I afford to lose that much?

If the answer to the second question is yes, the process stops at this point. If the question is answered no, then the process continues.

The magnitude of loss of each threat can be calculated using the following formula:

$$Loss\ due\ to\ threat = Average\ loss\ per\ threat\ occurrence\ \mathbf{1}$$
$$Frequency\ of\ loss\ occurrence$$

One must remember that this formula is a planning tool; it's not meant to produce highly precise results. Management uses this ballpark estimating concept in almost all other decisions. For example, when deciding whether to carry a new line of product, management decides how much the company will make by deciding the average selling price times the average amount sold. This concept is used to decide whether to carry a new product. It should not come as a surprise that the same concept is used in determining controls.

Let's look at an example of how we might use this in a threat situation. A typical threat that might concern us is that an employee will improperly calculate the amount a customer owes. We believe that customers will recognize when they are overcharged and bring this to the attention of our sales clerk, while if undercharged many customers will overlook it. We first estimate how much of a mistake the clerk is likely to make. Let us assume it will be $5. We then assume that each clerk will make this mistake once per day, for a loss per clerk of $25 a week, or approximately $1,250 per year. Having estimated the magnitude of the threat, we now have very valuable information, which tells us:

1. *Whether it is worth controlling.* For example, small losses are probably not worth controlling, while large ones are.
2. *How much we can spend for control.* In our clerk example, if we could reduce the loss to zero, we could spend up to $1,250 to do it. If we spent over $1,250, it would not be economical, but if we spent less than $1,250, it would be a cost-effective control. Examining this example might answer the question of whether to get a new, more sophisticated cash register.

Step 3 — Select the Control Solution

The calculation of the expected loss due to the threat tells us what our control solution should be. In our threat example of the employee underpricing the sales amount, we said that the frequency would be approximately 250 times per year and the average loss per occurrence $5. Since this is the formula to calculate the magnitude of the threat, and the objective of controls is to reduce the threat, then the formula tells us that we can reduce threats in only one of two ways:

1. Reduce the frequency of loss.
2. Reduce the average loss per occurrence.

In practice, we should address our controls at the larger of these two variables. If the frequency of occurrence is significantly greater relative to the amount of loss per occurrence, then we should control the frequency. If the loss is significantly greater relative the frequency, then we should control the loss. Let's look at some examples of how this works:

- *Example 1 — high frequency, low loss.* Our example of clerical errors in recording sales is an example of this type of problem. Therefore, most organizations direct their control at reducing the frequency of loss as opposed to the amount of the loss. For example, most fast-food chains install cash registers that have a picture of the product on it as opposed to the amount. If someone pushes the wrong button, the amount will be wrong, but that should occur much less frequently because the person at the register is pushing pictures instead of numbers.

- *Example 2 — high loss, low frequency.* An example in this category would be a fire. Fire occurs infrequently, but when it occurs the loss is very high. Therefore, we direct our controls at reducing the loss as opposed to reducing the frequency. Typical controls of this type are sprinkler systems, fire departments, fire extinguishers, and fire insurance. None of these reduces the frequency of fire, but should fire occur they all reduce the loss.

The types of controls that are directed toward reducing frequency of occurrence are:

- *Segregation of functions.* The task is divided into pieces so that if errors occur they should be picked up by the second or third group.
- *Redundancy.* The task is performed twice to make sure it is performed correctly.
- *Procedures/methods.* An individual is told to perform a task in a predetermined number of steps that are designed to reduce errors.
- *Authorization/approval.* A supervisor or manager must look at work to verify its correctness before it can be processed.

The types of controls that are oriented more toward reducing loss include:

- *Number systems.* These attempt to identify missing documents or assets.
- *Confirmation.* A customer, employee, or manager is asked to confirm that something happened, such as a customer saying, "I received the product," or an employee saying, "Inventory has arrived."
- *Reimbursement.* These are controls such as having insurance or taking a customer to small claims court for nonpayment of receivables to collect the funds.
- *Accountability.* Individuals are held accountable for their work.

Step 4 — Select the Method to Monitor the Control

We need to know that controls are working. The department of traffic monitors traffic lights to determine if they are giving too much or too little green light in each direction. Organizations must monitor their controls to determine that they are working effectively. For example, if the controls placed on the sales people are preventing them from taking orders and customers are walking away, the controls might need adjusting.

This step is performed by the manager asking the question: "How do I know that this control is working?" The method that will answer that question is the one that should be installed to monitor the effectiveness of control.

Examples of monitoring processes for controls include:

Control	Method to Know Control Works
Customer credit limit	The dollar amount of bad debts. If bad debts are too high, the creditlimit control is not working.
Inventory on hand	Stockouts. If stockouts are too high, there is not enough inventory on hand; if they are too low, there is probably too much inventory on hand.
Cash receipts from over-the-counter sales	Variance between recorded sales and cash in the register. If the variances are too great either way, there is a cash-collection control problem.

Step 5 — Implement the Control

The final step in the control process is implementation. The implementation normally goes smoothly if the previous steps have been performed. On the other hand, if the steps have been shortcut, the implementation process may meet resistance from those required to use it.

The implementation of a control should involve the following tasks:

• Explain to the users of the control the purpose of installing the control. People are more receptive to doing something when they understand why.
• Train the people involved in how to use the control.
• Train management on how to monitor whether or not the control is effective.
• Inform people as to when they are to begin using the control.
• Assign one person accountable for ensuring that the control is followed.

There is nothing magical or difficult about the control design process. It is just another process, like maintaining your automobile. If you follow the steps properly, the probability of poor automobile performance is significantly reduced. On the other hand, if you decide not to follow the process (that is, the controls), then you shouldn't be surprised when you have automotive problems. The same holds true with control design. If you do it by the steps, it works. If you shoot from the hip and throw controls at what you believe to be problems without doing your homework, the controls may not achieve your desired objective.

MANAGEMENT CONTROL PLAN OF ACTION

Control begins at the top and goes downward. If senior management wants control, it happens; if senior management does not consider control important, control is not viewed as important in the eyes of the employees.

Eight actions are required to create a strong control environment. These actions must be initiated by senior management, even though it will not be responsible for implementing all actions.

The four parties involved in control in any business are:

• Senior management
• Operating management
• Accountant
• Staff/employees

The eight management control actions, together with the individual having the primary or secondary responsibility for that action, are listed in Figure 3-7 and described below:

Control Action 1 - Create a Control Awareness Experience has shown that unless there is a supportive environment for control by senior management, good control will not exist. For example, if senior management is openly cheating on taxes, buying personal items with company funds, and tolerating control violations, a good control environment will not exist. Senior management can do much to create a good control environment by training operating management and its staff in what the control objectives are, how controls work, and how to develop control solutions.

Num-ber	Control Action	Chapter Refer-ence	Responsibility			
			Senior Manage-ment	Operating Manage-ment	Accoun-tant	Staff/ Employ-ees
1	Create a control awareness	1-3	P	S		
2	Identify threats to the business	1-11	P	S		
3	Develop and implement the method to identify variances	2	S		P	
4	Develop control strategies	3	P	S		
5	Assign control accountability	3	P	S		
6	Develop control solutions	3-11		P		
7	Operate controls	4-11		P		P
8	Monitor the effectiveness of controls	12-13	P	S	P	S

P = primary responsibility
S = secondary responsibility

Figure 3-7 MANAGEMENT PLAN OF ACTION FOR CONTROL

Control Action 2 – Identify Threats to the Business The primary responsibility for identifying what can go wrong resides with senior management, although operating management should be a contributor to this exercise.

Control Action 3 – Develop and Implement the Method to Identify Variances Small businesses cannot afford elaborate systems of control, nor can they depend on segregation of responsibilities to identify serious problems such as employee theft, mismanagement, or abuse. Therefore, small organizations must compensate by installing some general checks, such as the popcorn test, that provide reasonable assurance that the system is working properly. The detail controls then identify and correct the small problems.

Control Action 4 – Develop Control Strategies Senior management must decide how it wants to address control in the corporation. These strategies were discussed earlier in this chapter and included such issues as to whether or not to prosecute control violators. Management must have clearly established in its minds what it wants to do before it can expect the operating management and staff to properly execute the control solutions.

Control Action 5 – Assign Control Accountability Controls work best when a specific individual is assigned accountability for that control area. For example, if inventory is to be controlled, one person should be accountable. Senior management should make the accountability assignments.

Control Action 6 – Develop Control Solutions The accountable individual should develop a control solution for each identified threat.

Control Action 7 – Operate Controls The day-to-day operation of controls is the responsibility of operating management and staff. However, while the staff will execute the control, operating management should be held accountable and responsible for the proper execution of those controls.

Control Action 8 – Monitor the Effectiveness of Controls In larger organizations this is performed by internal auditors. In smaller organizations it must be performed by senior management. If a control monitoring method is established as part of the control design process, then monitoring becomes an easy step for senior management. The combination of the ripoff tests plus the monitoring information enables management to have reasonable assurance that the system of controls is working effectively.

CONTROL RULE OF THUMB 8
The fulfillment of management's control responsibility begins with a plan of action. It concludes when that plan of action is in place and working.

=II=
What needs controlling?

Controls are not something you "throw at" a problem. They should be designed to reduce identified threats that are of sufficient magnitude to be of concern to management.

4

controlling revenue-generating activities

Without revenue there is no business. Revenue generation is the most important function of a business. Some argue that payroll is the most important application, because without payroll there are no employees and thus no business. However, the majority of business people would probably subscribe to the opinion that revenue comes first.

This chapter begins to answer the question of what needs controlling. Considered are those activities within the organization that directly contribute to revenue generation: sales, billing, cash receipts, and product distribution. The purpose of this chapter is to provide advice on what parts of the revenue-generation activity need controlling. This objective is accomplished through asking and answering a series of questions about revenue-activity controls.

MANAGEMENT'S CONTROL QUESTIONS

For the purpose of answering the question, "What needs controlling?" the business has been divided into a series of controllable activities. By definition, an activity is a part of a business that can be controlled separately from the other parts of the business. Organizationally, the activity may involve two or more people or departments. Or, a single individual may control more than one activity. However, for control purposes, each activity can be dealt with as a stand-alone activity.

An automobile engine gives the appearance of being a single unit of activity. However, in servicing the engine, we can subdivide it into a series of activities, such as carburetor, starter, cooling system, generator, and cylinders. Just as each of these parts can be serviced independently, so can the activities discussed in Part II be controlled independently.

Each of the eight chapters covers a different controllable activity and is structured around the following series of control questions that management should consider:

1. *What is the management challenge?* Each of these activities poses some unique challenges to management. For example, in revenue generation, management needs to look for better ways to generate revenue. One of the objectives of control is to help management with these challenges.

2. *Why should I be concerned? (the threats).* These are the reasons the activities might not achieve management's expectations. In other words, these threats may cause losses in this activity.

3. *How should I structure my staff?* The key to control in a small business is people. If people are properly positioned within the activity, the strength of controls will increase and the probability of loss decrease.

4. *What are the key controls?* In each activity there are hundreds or maybe even thousands of controls. However, a few key controls can be relied on to provide an adequate level of control in each activity.

5. *What threats do the key controls address?* Management needs to know the key controls will address their concerns. This section of each chapter will identify which key controls address which threats.

6. *If I could only afford two controls, what should they be?* Controls cost money, but so do losses due to the absence of controls. Many managers are not believers in control. Therefore, this question attempts to respond to the manager who only wants to commit minimal resources to controls in activity in question.

7. *How do I know the controls work?* If the business expends time and effort developing and implementing controls, managers want some assurance that they are working. This question suggests some techniques and self-assessment methods to evaluate the effectiveness of the installed controls.

WHAT IS THE MANAGEMENT CHALLENGE IN REVENUE-GENERATION ACTIVITIES?

The revenue-generating activity, or *cycle* as it is sometimes called, produces the money necessary to drive the other business activities. The source of revenue generation varies from industry to industry. In retailing and wholesaling it's selling a product; in real estate it's selling property; in insurance it's selling policies; in consulting it's selling services; and in financial industry it's lending money. While each industry has different approaches to revenue generation, all industries share the following common management challenges (note that controls should support and not hinder these challenges):

1. *Attracting customers.* Through location of the business, advertising, third parties, or other means, the product of the business must be brought to the attention of potential customers.

2. *Competitive products.* The business must have and offer products that are equal to or better than other similar products in the marketplace in one manner or another. A product can be superior because it is built better, more conveniently located, comes with better service, has a lower price, and so on.

3. *Product line must be one for which there is a demand.* A product is sold only when there is a demand for it. As demand changes, so must the product line, location of business, or method of selling. Management must keep its pulse on the marketplace to ensure that the product line stays synchronized with customer needs.

4. *Continual customer loyalty.* Businesses generally survive because the same customers keep returning. Ensuring this customer loyalty requires the business to properly service that customer and to stand behind the quality of the product. The ability to return or exchange products is a policy designed to promote customer loyalty.

5. *Sufficient quantity of products on hand.* The business must have products available to meet the needs of the customers. While some customers may wait if the desired products are not in stock, many will go to other businesses to purchase them. This poses a real challenge to management: on-hand products for which demand decreases may result in unsalable merchandise, and overstocking will increase the cost of doing business.

CONTROL RULE OF THUMB 9
It is generally better to err on the side of too few controls than too many, since it is easier to add controls than to delete them.

WHY SHOULD I BE CONCERNED?
(THE THREAT)

Management has two major concerns over revenue activities. First, the activities may fail to generate sufficient revenue. Second, management may not collect all of the monies that should have been collected based on the sales. These general concerns can be translated into the following seven threats:

1. Product Shipped or Delivered but Not Billed   The customer receives the product but is not charged for the product. This can occur for any of the following reasons:

- Paperwork is lost after shipment so the billing never occurs.
- Invoice fails to include one or more items shipped.
- More items are shipped than billed.

2. Wrong Product Shipped   The customer orders one product but is given or shipped another. This is attributable to:

- Communication problems in understanding the product the customer wanted
- Inaccurate recording of the product wanted on the invoice/shipping memo
- Correct recording of the product on the shipping memo but delivery of the wrong product to the customer

   Losses can occur in two ways. First, the item shipped may be of more value than the one ordered, and the customer keeps it. Second, the customer returns it for the right product, and the business loses the cost of shipping the wrong product and then returning it to stock. If that wrong product shipment caused the company to be out of stock in that item, the company might also lose an unfulfilled sale.

3. Wrong Price Calculation   Revenue can be lost due to inaccurate or incomplete invoicing. This can occur because of:

- Wrong product being listed
- Wrong quantity being stated

- Wrong price being listed
- Wrong extension of price times quantity
- Wrong calculation of sales tax
- Wrong calculation of shipping charges
- Wrong accumulation of total due

4. Billed to Wrong Customer At the time of the sale and shipment, the invoice might be prepared for the wrong customer. This can occur because of:

- A communication problem between the customer and sales clerks
- Incorrect recording of the customer name
- Spoofing theft

Spoofing is a criminal technique in which one person causes another person to believe some event is true that in fact is not true. Companies accepting telephone orders are particularly vulnerable to spoofing. An individual calls pretending to be a regular customer and asks for a shipment to be ready for pickup by a messenger or delivered to a holding area in a place such as an airport. Organizations should be alert to this scam. If a customer order is unusual as far as day of order, type of product ordered, or quantity ordered, the business should call the customer back and confirm that the order is legitimate.

5. Wrong Cash Collection The sales clerk can accept the wrong amount of cash as payment in full for a purchase. While most of these errors are just dumb mistakes by the sales clerks, they can also happen as a result of con artist activity. Again, sales clerks should be alert to these types of activities. For example, a customer gives a sales clerk a $50 bill. As the sales clerk starts to make change, the customer asks for the $50 bill back and gives the clerk a $20 bill in its place. All this time, the customer is holding a running conversation with the clerk. The net result of the gimmick is that the customer gets change for a $50 bill, when actually a $20 has been given.

6. Cash Missing All of the cash collected during the revenue-generation activity may not be deposited in the business account. This might occur because:

- Cash is lost.
- Cash is taken by employees or customers.

7. Wrong Products Stocked   If a business stocks the wrong products or the wrong quantities of the right products, they stand to have large losses due to poor business practices. This is not the same type of loss associated with many of the other threats. The stocking of the wrong product can cause the business to lose monies in the following ways:

- Loss of sales because the desired product is not in stock
- Loss due to unsalable stock
- Perishable or dated stock (such as food, calendars, and so on) wasted because it becomes obsolete or rotten before it can be sold
- Interest carrying costs on excess inventory
- Cost of storage space for excessive inventory

     Some of these losses are controllable in the traditional sense, while others must be dealt with by management skills and intuition. Controls help match on-hand quantity with user demand. On the other hand, it is difficult for controls to determine which new products will sell, but controls can normally identify products whose sales are decreasing in time so that those products can be quickly depleted without large reorders.

CONTROL RULE OF THUMB 10
Controls should be established as early as possible in each activity.

HOW SHOULD I STRUCTURE MY STAFF?

Revenue generation involves the following four functions:

1. Order taking
2. Issuance/delivery of product
3. Collection of monies
4. Return or exchange of products

Type of business and business size permitting, these four functions should be performed by four different individuals or four different groups of people. In an ideally controlled environment, the following steps would occur:

1. A sales person would complete a prenumbered sales slip for the items purchased. One copy of the sales slip is retained by the sales person, one copy is sent to the warehouse for issuance of the product, and the remaining copies are given to the customer.

2. The customer takes his or her copies of the sales slip to the cashier, who recalculates the invoice mathematics and collects the funds from the customer. The cashier retains one copy of the sales slip and stamps the customer's copy paid.

3. The customer presents the sales slip marked paid to the shipping department, which gives the customer the product.

4. At the end of the day, a fourth person reconciles the three sales slips to ensure that what has been sold has been paid for and that what has been shipped has been paid for.

5. If a customer returns an item for a refund, the item is given to someone other than the person who will refund the monies. The receiver of the item issues a prenumbered credit memorandum.

6. The prenumbered credit memorandum is taken to the cashier, who in turn gives the customer any monies due. If the customer wants to exchange a product and there are no funds involved, the customer copy of the credit memo would be taken to the shipping department instead of the cashier to acquire a replacement product.

Many businesses cannot afford or are not set up to operate in this ideally controlled manner. For example, food stores and many retail stores have the same individual write the sales slip, collect the monies, and issue the merchandise. To guard employees from themselves in moments of weakness, the owner/manager should at least periodically:

- Watch for signals—nods, winks, and so on—between sales persons and customers, which might suggest collusion.
- Pay special attention to sales people when surrounded by a cluster of people.
- Be alert to the use of overring slips to cover cash shortages.

- Watch items bypassed when ringing up sales.
- Ensure that personal checks are not being used to cover shortages.
- Occasionally enlist the service of a professional shopper's firm to monitor the activities of sales people.

WHAT ARE THE KEY CONTROLS?

Businesses use hundreds of different controls in the revenue-generation area. Some of these controls are very sophisticated, such as those available with electronic cash registers and computers, while others are simple and straightforward.

The implementation of controls varies by the size of business and the sophistication of the equipment available to sales personnel. Some businesses use computer terminals to record sales. The same entry of data provides controls not only to the revenue-generation activities but also to credit, accounts receivable, inventory, and the inventory reorder process. However, rather than provide wrong lists of controls and a variety of implementation for each control, the approach taken in this book will be to describe the key controls.

A *key control* by definition is a very reliable control in the activity under discussion. Experience has shown that the proper implementation of a few key controls is more effective than a large number of less reliable controls. It is suggested that businesses, rather than "overkill" an area with extensive controls, should rely on the key controls. It is better to err on the side of too few controls than too many. Normally it is easier to add a control than to delete one.

The key controls in the revenue-generation activity are:

1. Formal and Timely Documentation of Sales Control over revenue means getting control as early as possible in the revenue cycle. The formal recording is a controlled recording of a sale. This can be accomplished using a prenumbered sales ticket or a cash register or other electronic recording device. Capturing the sale on a timely basis normally ensures control throughout the revenue-generation activity.

2. Formal and Timely Recording of Cash Many businesses sell their products for either cash or credit. Since cash is highly negotiable and desirable, it requires special controls. If cash is received by someone other than the sales person, it is recorded independently of sales. If it is received by the sales person, the sales document can document the receipt of cash.

3. Customer Confirmation Copy   Customers should be given a copy of the documentation recorded by the business. This control uses the customer as a control. Customers know what they ordered, what they paid, and what they were delivered. If the paperwork shows something different than what they ordered, paid, or were delivered, they frequently will bring this to the attention of the business. Owners and managers should be very concerned over variances between acts and paperwork. If customers do not get copies of the paperwork, sales people can record one item for paperwork purposes and charge the customer a higher amount for the product actually ordered. The sales person can then pocket the difference. However, while theft may be one of the reasons for loss, sloppy work practices also invariably result in losses to the business.

4. Authorization Needed to Move the Product   No merchandise or service should be available until the appropriate authorization has been approved. In most instances this will be a copy of the sales slip or payment indication for the product or service.

5. All Cash Deposited Intact   All cash received from revenue generation should be assembled and deposited intact. It is normally advisable to deposit cash daily. If cash is removed to pay for product deliveries or other purposes, it becomes difficult to reconcile cash received through revenue generation with cash deposited in the bank. The full intact deposit of cash enables management to account for cash receipts.

6. Reconciliation of Sales, Billing, Cash Receipts, and Deposits   Management should be able to account for all the revenue generated from sales. At a minimum, this is a reconciliation between sales and cash deposits in the bank. However, if sales are made on credit, then there will be a delay in cash receipts. In that case, the reconciliation will be made to the funds recorded in the accounts receivable system (see Chapter 5).

7. Formal Recording of Returns Management must determine a policy on product returns. Generally, organizations are under no obligation to either exchange products or return the purchase price to the customer. However, in order to retain customer loyalty, most organizations have at least a minimal policy on returning products. Because this process authorizes the distribution of cash, it should be closely controlled. Some of the product return concerns include the following situations:

- Cash is paid out, but no product is returned.
- Cash paid out is for a higher price than the product was purchased for.
- The returned product was sold by a different business.
- The returned product is damaged and cannot be restored to inventory.

The formal recording of returns by someone other than the normal sales person or cashier is a strong control. The formal recording document should become the basis of crediting a customer's account, returning monies to the customer, as well as of controlling the returned product. If the product returned is of no value or the credit is the result of a dispute, then it is recommended that a manager approve the return.

8. Sales Analysis The objective of the sales analysis control is to evaluate the effectiveness of the revenue-generation activity. Specifically, sales analysis can provide data for revenue activities such as:

- *Sales by sales person*—to determine individual sales productivity
- *Sales by product or product line*—to determine the viability of continuing to sell a specific product or product line
- *Need to reorder*—determined by establishing reorder points based on sales
- *Determining reorder size*—to establish the amount of each product to be ordered
- *Location of sales*—to indicate which area or store (if more than one available) is most productive in selling which product

- *Sales by customer*—to indicate which customers are buying and not buying as a basis for advertising and sales promotion campaigns

Sales analysis can also show profitability, which will be covered in Chapter 10.

WHAT THREATS DO THE KEY CONTROLS ADDRESS?

The control-design approach begins with threat identification. Management then decides which threats warrant the implementation of controls. Having identified the threats, management must then know which controls are effective against reducing which threats.

This and the following chapters will include a matrix showing the relationship in each activity between the threats and the key controls described in that chapter. Figure 4-1 is the matrix for reducing the threats in the revenue-generation activities. The checkmarks in the matrix show which key controls are most effective in reducing which threats.

Use the matrix by first selecting the threats that need to be reduced. Then scan that column in the matrix to determine which of the key controls are effective in reducing that threat. For example, if the business is concerned that products will be shipped or delivered but not billed, then the two controls you might select are (1) formal and timely documentation of sales and (2) authorization needed to move product.

Implicit in the matrix but not directly stated are the threat formula variables. As mentioned in Chaper 3, a threat can be reduced by reducing either the frequency of occurrence of that threat or the average loss per occurrence. The matrix helps explain which threat variable is most apparent for each threat. This can be determined by evaluating the key controls for each threat. For example, for the "product shipped or delivered but not billed," the identified key controls address the frequency rather than the amount of the loss. Therefore, you can assume that the effective controls for reducing this threat should be aimed at reducing the frequency as opposed to the amount of the loss. This is important should a business want to select or use a control not in the matrix.

Key Controls \ Threats	Product Shipped or Delivered but Not Billed	Wrong Product Shipped	Wrong Price Calculation (e.g., Wrong Product Quantity or Price)	Billed to Wrong Customer	Wrong Cash Collection	Cash Missing	Stocked Wrong Products
Formal and timely documentation of sales	✔						
Formal and timely recording of cash					✔	✔	
Customer confirmation copy		✔	✔	✔	✔	✔	
Authorization needed to move product	✔	✔					
All cash deposited intact						✔	
Reconciliation of sales, billings, cash receipts, and deposit					✔	✔	
Formal recording of returns						✔	
Sales analysis							✔

Figure 4-1   REVENUE GENERATION THREAT-REDUCTION MATRIX

However, the type of product and the type of business may change the threat characteristic. For example, the items shipped may be very few in quantity and large in value. In these cases organizations may embellish some of the key controls in order to reflect that difference. For example, if the sales documentation required one or more levels of approval before the sale was finalized, then the key control would address not only frequency but also loss.

IF I CAN ONLY AFFORD TWO CONTROLS, WHAT SHOULD THEY BE?

The two key controls for revenue generation are:

- Formal and timely documentation of sales
- Reconciliation of sales, billing, receipts, and deposit

Recording the sale at the point where it occurs grabs control of revenue at the starting point of the cycle. Reconciling those sales to billings, cash receipts, and deposits provides assurance that the cycle is completed with reasonable accuracy and completeness.

In control language this is frequently referred to as the *two-out-of-three control*. Control addresses input, processing, and output. These two selected key controls address the revenue activities at the point of input and the point of output. They do not address the revenue processing and thus may be vulnerable in that wrong products may be shipped and so on. On the other hand, at minimal cost they provide maximum control.

HOW DO I KNOW THE CONTROLS WORK?

Management has a responsibility to verify that the controls are in place and functioning. Two methods will be suggested to management for this purpose. The first are some generalized tests that can be performed to provide some assurance that the total amounts included in revenue activities are correct. In accounting terms these are called *substantive tests* because they test the reasonableness of the amounts recorded on the financial statements. These are point-in-time tests, in that they only test the reasonableness of the financial amount at a specific point in time or for a period of time such as a month.

The second type of test is a control-oriented test, which makes sure that the controls are in place and working continuously. This type of test is directed at determining that the control itself is functioning, rather than the fact that the proper amount of funds have been recorded. It assumes that if the control is functioning correctly the proper amounts will be recorded.

In practice, it is the totality of the two methods that provides assurance that the controls are functioning. For each activity, management will be provided these methods, and the overall approach for using the methods will be described in Chapter 12.

Substantive Tests

The tests that management can undertake to verify that the revenue financial amounts are reasonable include:

- *Popcorn test.* Compare the amount of revenue generated to some other business characteristic that can be used to verify the reasonableness of revenue.
- *Gross-profit test.* The amount of products sold is multiplied by the average selling price to see whether the total revenue recorded is reasonable. This method must be modified to take into account any product returns, discounts, or other means of varying recorded revenue.
- *Period-to-period comparison.* Revenue generated in one accounting period is compared to revenue in a previous accounting period. In businesses that have yearly fluctuations, this frequently involves comparing the current months activity to the same month in the previous year, or comparing this month to last month. Also, revenue may be broken into categories such as services performed or product lines. Variances that appear unusual should be investigated.

Internal Control Self-Assessment Checklist

Checklists are comprised of a series of self-assessment questions. The questions included in this book have been designed to be self-explanatory. However, Murphy tells us that whatever can go wrong will go wrong. This means that there may be typographical errors, sentences with words reversed, and possibly, although it's hard to admit, some of the questions may be poorly worded. The purpose of this mini-sermon is that if you do not understand the question, please discard it. There should be enough comprehensible questions left to provide a reasonable assessment of the adequacy of controls.

The manager should answer the questions on the checklist. If uncertain as to the answer, the manager should undertake an investigation. The comments column should be used to explain no answers and qualify yes answers.

Checklist 1 is designed to help managers assess the adequacy of controls over the revenue-generation activities. The checklist is struc-

| | | Response | | |
Item	Yes	No	N/A	Comments
1. Have procedures been established for the acceptance and approval of orders for nonstandard terms, services, or unusual delivery arrangements?				
2. Has a policy been established on the approval of customer checks and use of credit cards?				
3. Has a policy been established on product warranties and returned goods?				
4. Are customer complaints channeled through someone other than the individual responsible for customer service and billing?				
5. Are checks of quantities of goods shipped made prior to shipments, such as double-counting shipments?				
6. Is there a control over cash receipts, such as prenumbered cash receipt forms or order forms?				
7. Is there a segregation of duties between access to cash receipts and keeping records of sales, customer credits, cash receipts, and accounts receivable?				
8. Are cash receipts promptly recorded?				
9. Are sales promptly recorded?				
10. Are cash receipts reconciled with bank deposits?				
11. Are all shipped orders billed?				

Checklist 1 REVENUE-GENERATION SELF-ASSESSMENT

tured so that *yes* questions are considered to be good control practices and no questions poor control practices. If a particular item on the checklist is not applicable to the business, check the N/A (not applicable) column.

The items answered *no* to, as well as some with qualified *yes* answers, represent vulnerabilities. A vulnerability is a weakness in control that may permit a loss to occur. Management should investigate these areas and strengthen controls as appropriate.

CONTROL RULE OF THUMB 11
If controls are burdensome and time consuming, they are not effective. Controls should improve the process, not hinder it.

5

controlling credit, receivables, and collections

Most organizations would prefer to have all payments made in cash at the time of the sale. This would eliminate maintaining records on collections, losing the interest on monies awaiting collection, and frequently having to badger customers to collect funds. The reason for selling on credit is simple—it improves sales. It is more convenient for customers to buy on credit than to pay cash.

This chapter discusses the balance between granting credit to improve sales and losing revenue because of the failure to collect receivables. The concerns involved with receivables are discussed, together with the controls that can be used to reduce those threats. The chapter concludes with the methods management can use to ensure that the company's credit, receivables, and collection activities are adequately controlled.

WHAT IS THE MANAGEMENT CREDIT, RECEIVABLES, AND COLLECTIONS ACTIVITY CHALLENGE?

Whether or not to allow customers to purchase on credit is one of the most important financial and managerial decisions facing the owner or manager of a small business. The reasons most commonly cited by small businesses for granting credit to customers include:

1. Credit sales are easier to make than cash sales.
2. Customers tend to buy more products when using credit than when paying cash. The net result is they spend more money at the store.
3. Customer loyalty is strengthened by offering the convenience of credit sales.

The dilemma facing the small business is whether it is more beneficial to offer credit and increase sales than it is to pay the collection costs and lose sales. The answer to that question will depend on:

1. Type and cost of products sold
2. Integrity and credit standing of company's customers
3. Industry credit collection records
4. Management's interest in granting customers credit

The disadvantages that the small business should consider prior to establishing a business credit policy are that:

1. Working capital is tied up in the form of receivables.
2. Accounting costs are required to check credit and collect receivables.
3. Customers frequently abuse the privilege of returning goods when those goods can be charged.
4. Higher prices must be charged to cover the additional costs of uncollectible accounts, return of damaged goods, and potential repossession of products.
5. Some customers will overestimate their purchasing power and default on payments, which will result in either losses or extended collection periods.

WHY SHOULD I BE CONCERNED?
(THE THREATS)

A large percentage of the cash receipts of many corporations flows through accounts receivable. The collectibility of the receipts is dependent on how well the credit and collection functions perform. At least one major corporation has lost its current accounts receivable file; as a result the corporation ended the year in a loss position and nearly went into bankruptcy.

Many smaller corporations get into severe cash-flow problems because of the slow collection of their receivables. This is particularly true when small corporations deal with very large corporations. The small companies have a tendency not to pressure their customers because they are afraid of losing receivables. So they continue to extend their own credit position and may end up borrowing money or factoring their receivables. The net result of this may be the loss of profit on those sales whose receivables were factored or several months overdue.

The concerns in the credit, receivables, and collections activities are:

1. Customer Will Not Pay for Charge Sales   It is normally easy to sell items on credit. No cash is involved, just the customer's word or signature on a document. In many smaller businesses the customer is not even required to sign a document indicating purchase of the item. The challenge for the business comes in collecting the funds.

Books could be written on the reasons customers do not pay their credit charges, including:

- The customer going out of business
- The customer going into bankruptcy
- The customer stating the products were defective
- The customer being in a serious cash bind, asking for an extension on payments, and then never making the payments

2. Collections Will Not Be Timely   The higher the bank prime rate, the more difficult it is to get collections from customers. Customers want to keep their money as long as possible in order to earn maximum interest in their cash accounts. Without good collection policies and follow-up, the delays in payment may seriously affect the business. Among the reasons customers cite for paying late are:

- "We never received a statement."
- "The check was mailed; it must have been lost in the mail."
- "We're waiting on a large check from one of our customers."

- "It is our policy not to pay until X days after receipt of statement."
- "The invoice was mislaid; please send another one."
- "The person who signs the checks is on vacation (or sick)."
- "Our dog ate the invoice."

3. Accounts Will Be Lost   A credit sale is normally documented on a piece of paper. If that paper is lost, the record of the sale is lost. If the receivable is recorded on the computer and the computer file is lost, the receivable is lost. It is surprising how few customers remember that they owe you money when you are unable to substantiate the receivable.

A receivable can be lost at any of the following points:

- When the sale occurs
- When it is transmitted to the accounts receivable recording function
- When it is in the accounts receivable file

4. Receipts Will Be Lost   The collections for receivables may be given or transferred by customers to the business but never get deposited in the bank. This can happen through any of the following:

- Carelessness
- Employee theft
- Theft by a third party
- Loss in transit between the customer and the company, in which case the customer believes it is paid (a disputed collection)

5. Sales Will Be Lost Due to Tight Credit Policy   The dilemma faced by the business person is whom to give credit to and how much credit to grant. If the company refuses credit, customers may be lost. On the other hand, if credit is too loose, the business may be giving products away because it will not be able to collect the receivables.

CONTROL RULE OF THUMB 12
Many corporations have gone bankrupt due to lax credit policies, but very few have gone under due to tight credit policies.

HOW SHOULD I STRUCTURE MY STAFF?

The credit, receivables, and collections activity is comprised of three separate functions. Ideally structured, these functions would be performed by three separate people, as follows:

1. Approval of Credit The individual who issues credit to customers should be a member of management. In small businesses this is frequently done by the owner or manager of the business. In larger organizations this may be delegated to the comptroller or financial officer of the organization. This individual should conduct a background check prior to issuing credit and then monitor credit to determine whether it should be increased, decreased, or canceled.

2. Maintain Accounts Receivable Records The maintenance of the accounts receivable records should be performed by someone who has responsibility for neither approving credit nor collecting the cash. If the business has an accountant or bookkeeper, this is a logical function for that individual. The function involves the following tasks:

- Posting billings to the customer accounts
- Preparing customer statements on a scheduled basis
- Posting payments to the customer account
- Aging the accounts receivable file and perhaps following up on delinquent accounts (in some instances done personally by the owner when some of the more important customers are delinquent)
- Writing off bad debts or adjust customers' accounts for other than payment or returned items (normally done only after authorization by a member of management)

3. Collections on Receivables The cash received on accounts should be handled by someone who is not responsible for record keeping. In many businesses the owner or manager opens the mail and thus receives the cash. In larger organizations this may be done by the mail room, which is normally instructed to endorse the checks restrictively and then separate them from the paperwork; the checks are then sent to whoever deposits the funds in the bank, and the paperwork goes to the accounts receivable posting function.

WHAT ARE THE KEY CONTROLS?

There are three general categories of controls. These are preventive, detective, and corrective. *Preventive controls* stop an event from occurring, *detective controls* uncover the fact that an unfavorable event has occurred, and *corrective controls* provide the means needed to correct an unfavorable event once it has occurred.

Let's look at an example of these three control categories. For the purpose of our example, let us assume that the threat we are attempting to control is fire. Preventive controls would include using fireproof materials, building firewalls, or prohibiting smoking in a building. Detective controls would include installing a fire alarm or smoke detector. And corrective controls for the threat of fire would include sprinkler systems, fire extinguishers, and the fire department.

Preventive, detective, and corrective controls can all be used to reduce the threats associated with the credit, receivables, and collections activities. Let's look at some examples. A background credit check is a preventive control; follow-up on delinquent accounts is a detective control; and, in the event that the original receivable records are lost, keeping duplicate accounts receivable records is a corrective control.

The key controls effective in reducing the credit, receivables, and collections activity threats are:

1. Set up a Customer Credit Verification Policy The businesses should have a credit policy. The policy should be directed at maximizing sales while minimizing risk and other associated credit costs. The policy should state:

- Who is eligible to acquire credit
- Who issues credit
- How credit will be approved
- How credit will be monitored and adjusted

The first step in extending credit is a careful selection of the customers to whom credit will be extended. It is generally good policy to have each customer make a written application on which sufficient background information is provided to make a credit reference check. Many businesses become members of credit bureaus in order to have customer credit verified. On the basis of this background analysis, a credit limit should be set for each customer. The customer should be told of the limit and other credit terms applicable to the customer's account. The credit limit and terms should be enforced.

2. Establish and Enforce Credit Limit   The credit policy should define the maximum amount of credit a customer can have. Before products are sold on credit, it should be determined whether or not the customer has already used his or her credit limit. If the current purchase will cause the customer to exceed the credit limit, then special authorization from a manager should be obtained. Organizations might also decide to suspend credit if customers' accounts are over sixty days old.

Businesses that have computers can use computerized authorization to issue credit. Many stores use a computer to provide their sales personnel with yes-no credit decisions. A simpler method is to develop a list of customers who have preapproved credit. The list should be monitored by management; as customers exceed or approach their credit limit, their names should be removed from the list or flagged for management approval before credit can again be issued.

3. Age Receivables and Follow up on Collections   Despite stringent credit policies and enforcement of credit limits, some accounts will inevitably become delinquent. It is important to know as soon as possible when this happens, because the older an account becomes, the more difficult it is to collect on.

The best method for preventing delinquent accounts is to enforce credit policies rigidly. Other good collection methods include the following:

1. Provide a discount for prompt payment of receivables.
2. Initially avoid high-pressure tactics to collect receivables. Frequently it is better to let the company owner act as the collection agent because the owner best realizes the value of maintaining goodwill with the customers.
3. Do not allow customers to take time paying receivables. The more time you give, the more difficult it is to collect the receivables.
4. Periodically examine the percentage of credit sales that ultimately become uncollectible. A high percentage may indicate the need for a tighter credit policy.

5. Include a personal note at the bottom of the regular monthly statement informing the customer that his or her account is delinquent and that its collection is important to the business.

6. Write a special collection letter to the customer using the following writing guidelines:

- Limit the letter to three or four sentences at most.
- Phrase the letter in such a way as to enlist the customer's cooperation, not to let off steam.
- If you are sending a series of letters over time to a given customer, try to make each one appeal to a different motive for paying, such as courtesy, pride, or, as a last resort, fear. Concentrate on only one motive per letter.
- If the customer is given alternatives, spell out what the customer can do, such as pay on account, call to make specific arrangements, settle within a certain time, and so on.
- Be consistent. Do not bargain or even hint of bargaining.
- Don't make statements or threats that can't be carried out. Be firm, but be reasonable and not antagonistic.
- Don't give the client any reasons for not paying. If the letter begins, "I know this has been a rough year," this provides the customer a logical reason for not paying the bill now or in the next few weeks.

If the normal approaches to collecting the money fail, the business at a minimum should stop selling on credit to that customer. It is better to lose the sale than to lose the product being sold. Customers that are poor at paying should not be considered good customers, and the business should not feel bad losing them.

CONTROL RULE OF THUMB 13
Let the nonpaying customers buy from your competitors. This increases your competitors' sales and increases your profitability.

Some of the methods that can be used to collect difficult-to-collect accounts include:

- Taking the customer to small claims court
- Turning the collectible over to a collection agency
- Factoring the accounts receivable
- Repossessing the property

4. Reconcile Sales on Credit, Accounts Receivable, and Collections   Accounts receivable normally interconnects two other activities. The invoicing system creates the receivables, and the cash collection system deletes them. Handling receivables by itself is primarily a record-keeping activity. Therefore, controls should assure that the record keeping is correct. This is accomplished through a reconciliation between invoicing, cash payments, and receivables using a simple accounting proof.

A simple accounting proof of receivables follows:

- *Start*: beginning accounts receivable balances
- *Add*: purchases made on credit
- *Subtract*: payments
- *Subtract*: adjustments to accounts receivable such as writeoffs
- *Equals*: ending accounts receivable balance

The reconciliation process should prove that the additions to receivables are the same as the charged sales for that period. It should also prove that the reductions from receivables equal the cash collections plus any other authorized reductions to receivables. Using this process, the individual maintaining the accounts receivable records will be assured that the record keeping is correct.

5. Establish Writeoff Authorization   A recorded account receivable is like money in the bank if it is collected. If the receivable is written off the books, money is lost. Therefore, writeoffs to accounts receivable should only occur when approved by management. Unless the amount is very small, this usually means approval by the owner or manager of the business.

6. Maintain and Reconcile Customer Accounts to the Total Accounts Receivable Balance   The financial statements of the business indicate the total accounts receivable due. This balance is normally obtained using the simple accounting proof described in the previous control. It is a master account and uses the totals of billings and collections to arrive at a new balance. Therefore, it is important to total the detailed receivables periodically—at least monthly—to ensure agreement with the accounts receivable balance.

7. Use National Credit Cards   Many businesses choose not to use their own credit system but rather the credit system of one of the banks. Mastercard and Visa are the two most commonly used credit systems. This eliminates the need for the business to establish credit, maintain receivables records, or wait for the collection of cash. However, there is a service charge associated with this of approximately 5 percent; moreover, some business customers may not have business Mastercard or Visa accounts. However, it does provide a business's customers the option of charging accounts without the risk of noncollections and it avoids the bookkeeping required when the business maintains its own accounts receivable.

CONTROL RULE OF THUMB 14

If no credit purchases become uncollectible, your credit policy is too tight. On the other hand, if too many receivables become uncollectible, your credit policies are too loose.

WHAT THREATS DO THE KEY CONTROLS ADDRESS?

Small businesses should carefully select the controls that they choose to install. A few well-placed controls generally do the job. Control concepts dictate that some losses should be considered acceptable. Generally, after the installation of a few key controls, the addition of other controls is not cost-effective. Controls need not be expensive when done properly.

The purpose of matching key controls to threats is to identify which controls reduce which threat. It is important in the control design process to clearly identify the threats before controls are installed. The key controls in the credit, receivables, and collections activities that reduce the threats within that activity are listed in Figure 5-1. This matrix can be

Key Controls \ Threats	Customer Will Not Pay for Charge Sales	Collections Will Not Be Timely	Accounts Will Be Lost	Receipts Will Be Lost	Sales Will Be Lost Due to Tight Credit Policy
Set up a customer credit verification policy	✔				✔
Establish and enforce credit limit	✔				✔
Age receivables and follow up on collections		✔			
Reconcile sales on credit, accounts receivable, and collections			✔	✔	
Establish writeoff authorization				✔	
Maintain and reconcile customer accounts to the total accounts receivable balance			✔		
Use national credit cards	✔	✔			✔

Figure 5-1 CREDIT, RECEIVABLES, AND COLLECTIONS THREAT-REDUCTION MATRIX

used by the individual accountable for controls in this area to reduce the threats that warrant attention.

IF I CAN ONLY AFFORD TWO CONTROLS, WHAT SHOULD THEY BE?

The type and extent of controls should vary from business to business and activity to activity. For example, in some organizations, receivables involve thousands of customers and are a significant part of the revenue of the organization. In other companies, receivables involve only a few key customers and do not take much time and effort. The type of controls, therefore, varies with the importance of the application, the number of transactions processed, and in the case of collections the delinquency of payment and the percentage of writeoffs.

The objective of suggesting two key controls is to aid the company where this activity is small in scope or the business is small. If only two controls can be used for the credit, receivables, and collections activities, the two recommended controls would be:

1. *Aging of receivables and collections follow-up*. Businesses cannot afford to let receivables sit on their books for an extended period of time because of the value of money. The two major concerns a business should have about delinquent accounts are (1) the older the account, the less the probability that it will ever be collected, and (2) the business may continue to sell products on credit to customers whose accounts are overdue and as a result may be increasing the amount of uncollectible receivables. While this control will not restrict credit to the best customers or establish credit limits—both of which are desirable—it will limit losses and help improve collections.

2. *Maintaining and reconciling customer accounts to the total accounts receivable balance*. The objective of this control is to prevent the loss of individual customer accounts receivable items. This is a relatively inexpensive control; it need be performed only once or twice a month; and it has the additional side benefit of reconciling accounts receivable to sales on credit and collections. This is because the accounts receivable balance should be calculated independently of the posting of detailed items to the accounts receivable file.

HOW DO I KNOW THE CONTROLS WORK?

The business should have two major concerns over the adequacy of accounts receivable controls: that the receivables will not be collectible and that they will be lost. Receivables can be lost through error, omission, or theft. The controls against lost receivables are effective against all three causes.

Putting controls in place is not enough. The owner or manager of the business has an obligation to periodically verify the proper functioning of the controls. Unless this responsibility is fulfilled, the control responsibility of senior management will not be properly executed.

Senior management should perform two types of control assessments. The first is substantive tests aimed at verifying the correctness of the accounts receivable balance. The second tests that the in-place controls work. As discussed in the previous chapter, the controls are expected to be working every day of the week, every hour of the day, in order to be considered reliable. If so, they provide assurance to the owner that the business transactions covered by the controls will be properly processed.

Substantive Tests

The substantive tests that the owner can perform to verify the correctness of the credit, receivables, and collections activities are:

1. Sniff Test   Owners should be aware of any changing credit purchase activities of customers or difficulties occurring in the collection activities. While it is difficult to say exactly what these problems are, owners who are on top of the credit purchasing and collection activities should be able to "smell" problems occurring. Examples of events that may appear unusual include:

- *Customers significantly increasing the amount of product they purchase on credit.* This may mean that the customer is having financial problems and other organizations have reduced or stopped selling the customer product on credit.
- *Collections for customers slowing down.* This occurs when interest rates go up or business conditions decrease. Your customers may be having problems collecting from their customers and thus are slower in paying. This may signal the owner to tighten credit policies and push collections.
- *Calls to customers about delinquent collections going unanswered.* When businesses start to get into trouble financially, they stop answering calls about delinquent accounts. This is a signal to take the customer to court, factor the receivable, or turn it over to a collection agency. Businesses that wait too long to collect their monies may

receive only a few cents on the dollar many months or even years later when bankruptcy suits are finally resolved.

As the owner gains experience in receivables and collections, he or she usually improves in using the sniff test to identify problems. It is an important test for a small business, which frequently knows the customers, the market, and the community well. This test provides early indicators of problems and can help avoid business losses.

2. Writeoffs/Credit-Memo Test   The business should continually monitor the percentage of receivables that are written off as uncollectible and the percentage of receivables that are satisfied by providing customers with credit memos against their receivables. It is good to identify the credit memo by cause. Reasons for issuing customers credit against their accounts receivable balance are returned goods, disputed charges, damaged goods, and after-the-fact price concessions. This test is particularly important when the owner or manager is not the individual who is authorizing the writeoffs or credits. These should be examined at specific points in time and for trends over a period of time. If the trend is upward for either of these ratios, the owner should be concerned.

3. Confirm Balances to Customers   Periodically, the owner should put a small note in the accounts sent to customers. The objective of the note is to determine from the customer whether or not the amount being billed is correct. The note should say something like, "We thank you for your business. We are in the process of ensuring that our records are correct and would appreciate your advising our president (or other officer, as long as it is not the individual maintaining the accounts receivable records) if the attached statement is incorrect." This type of confirmation is used in businesses by auditors and has proven to be a very effective practice. You must remember that it would not be difficult for one of your employees to pocket cash from a customer and record that as a credit sale. Since inquiries would normally go to the accounts receivable person, that individual could easily explain it as an error or keep that balance on the records of the organization but never bill the customer. It is even possible that fictitious customers could be on the books with balances that stay open forever. If this practice is used, the owner should accumulate the total of all of the statements being sent out to ensure that they are equal to the accounts receivable balance on the

Item	Response			
	Yes	No	N/A	Comments
1. Has a policy been established on who will be given credit and when?				
2. Are potential credit customers investigated for creditworthiness before credit is approved for them?				
3. Does each customer have a predefined credit limit?				
4. Have procedures been established for approving bad-debt writeoffs and other credits to customers' accounts?				
5. Are accounts receivable detailed customer records regularly reconciled to the general ledger?				
6. After the accounts receivable statements are prepared, are they mailed by someone other than the individual preparing the statements?				
7. Is there a restrictive endorsement of checks on receipt?				
8. Is appropriate follow-up action taken on overdue receivables?				
9. Are accounts receivables aged at least monthly?				
10. Are two individuals always present when mail is opened that contains cash or checks?				
11. Do you have a policy that all accounts receivable written off as uncollectible must be approved by management other than the individual responsible for maintaining accounts receivable?				
12. Are receivables billed to customers on a regular basis?				
13. Are receivables accepted only for customers who have not exceeded their credit limit or whose accounts are not in arrears?				

Checklist 2   CREDIT, RECEIVABLES,
AND COLLECTIONS SELF-ASSESSMENT

financial records. The owner should then personally mail the letters and instruct the staff to give the owner any envelopes returned by the post office as undeliverable. In addition, the owner should scan the customer accounts to ensure that they all appear to be legitimate.

Internal Control Self-Assessment Checklist

The evaluation of the adequacy of controls can be achieved through the use of a self-assessment checklist (see Checklist 2). This is the same process used by auditors to verify the adequacy of the system of controls in the business being audited. The objective of the process is to identify potential vulnerabilities. No answers to the checklist questions represent potential vulnerabilities and should be investigated by the owner or manager to determine whether it would be helpful to add or strengthen the controls. Checklist 2 should be used at least once per year.

CONTROL RULE OF THUMB 15
Guard your receivables as you would cash in your cash box. They are equally valuable.

6

controlling the purchasing-and-payables activity

One of the main uses of the business's cash is to purchase merchandise or products for resale. Lowering the amount paid out in purchasing merchandise usually raises the company's gross profit margin. To lower purchasing costs, the owner or manager must make sure that the business is taking advantage of all possible price breaks and discounts. The information necessary to establish this control is provided by establishing an up-to-date list of suppliers, costs, and details of past purchases. Times of the year when suppliers offer seasonal trade discounts should be specifically noted.

This chapter discusses the threats and controls applicable to the purchasing-and-payables activity, which, with the possible exception of payroll, will be the major use of the business's funds. Good controls are needed to ensure that the funds are properly used and that losses do not occur due to errors, omissions, or theft. The chapter offers some immediately implementable solutions to the purchasing and payables threats, as well as tests the owner can undertake to verify whether the controls are functioning properly.

WHAT IS THE MANAGEMENT PURCHASING-AND-PAYABLES ACTIVITY CHALLENGE?

The resources required to run the business are acquired through the purchasing activity. Each dollar spent through this activity is one less dollar of bottom-line profit. On the other hand, failure to acquire the right resources will affect the volume of sales and thus bottom-line profitability. Therefore, the owner's challenge is to walk a tightrope, buying neither too little or too much of what's needed to make the company successful.

Most of us have an attic or cellar full of junk. Much of this junk is past purchases we didn't need, didn't like getting, or no longer have a use for. Businesses fall into this same purchasing trap. Sales people are constantly knocking on the door tempting you to buy products you don't need, don't really want, or won't find much use for.

A good purchasing activity is a well-planned activity. We should only buy from shopping lists that result from a business plan. Obviously, a few emergencies will arise, causing exceptions to this rule. This does not make the rule invalid. These exceptions should relate to changes in plans that are not yet reflected in the purchasing plan. Examples are: product X is selling much faster than expected and must be reordered on an emergency basis, or a customer requires a special order. What the plan is designed to do is reduce or eliminate "impulse" purchases.

The specific purchasing-and-payables activity challenges that face the business are:

- *Ordering needed products.* The business must attempt through planning to determine precisely what is needed. These plans must be measured against business activities to ensure that they are consistent with the marketplace and other needs of the business. For example, if sales in a particular product are not going according to plan, then purchases should be adjusted accordingly. What the business must avoid is buying products for resale that are not selling, purchasing products for use in operating the business that are not needed, or buying products not needed in the quantities purchased.

- *Ordering in economic quantities.* Businesses should be alert to points at which they get price breaks, to sale times during the year offered by their suppliers, and to those suppliers selling the product at the lowest price. Reductions in the cost of item purchased reflect directly on bottom-line profits. A dollar saved on purchasing is equivalent to a dollar profit earned on sales. Purchasing at the lowest possible price requires the business to keep records on the best vendors, times, and quantities for ordering product. However, these must be consistent with the needs of the business.

- *Minimizing storage and carrying costs.* Inventory sitting on the shelves is not earning money for the business. Sometimes businesses become penny wise and pound foolish. For example, to save a few pennies per item, a company might buy in large quantity. However, that quantity may last the business for a year or even longer. When the interest and other carrying charges are added to the cost of the items purchased, and the potential obsolescence of that product is considered, it may have been cheaper to pay more and buy in smaller quantities. Note that some vendors will permit you to buy in large quantities and will store the product for you, and may not even bill you until you take delivery of the product.

Larger businesses hire purchasing agents. This is a highly specialized area if one wants to get the best possible product, in the most economic order quantity, and at the lowest possible price. In a smaller business the owner may be the purchasing agent. Regardless of who performs the function, the purchasing agent should acquire some basic training in purchasing, even if it is only reading a textbook. The potential savings between good purchasing practices and poor purchasing practices can make a significant difference in the profitability of the business.

WHY SHOULD I BE CONCERNED? (THE THREATS)

Threats are ever-present conditions that can lead to losses. It's important to recognize that threats cannot be eliminated, only controlled. Thus it becomes important to businesses to fully understand the threats to their business.

The specific threats of concern in the purchasing-and-payables activity are:

1. Paying for Product Not Received The objective of the purchasing function is to buy products. This assumes that the product paid for will be received by the business. Some of the reasons this may not happen are that:

- The product is shipped to the wrong customer.
- The product is never shipped.

- The product gets lost in transit.
- An employee has the business pay for personal purchases.
- The wrong product is delivered.
- The wrong quantity is delivered.

2. Paying Twice for Product   The payables system should issue checks for approved invoices or statements. Most businesses pay on predetermined days of the month. In this process, it is possible to pay for the same product twice for any of the following reasons:

- The business pays for the invoice and then pays again for the statement that includes the paid invoice.
- A vendor bills twice, so the business pays twice.
- An invoice is paid but not voided, then reentered into the payables system and paid again.

In many instances the vendor will recognize duplicate payments and refund the duplicate payment or credit the customer's account. However, just as some businesses are fouled up and pay invoices twice, other businesses are fouled up on the collections side and may not be aware that a particular item was paid twice.

3. Purchasing Unauthorized Product   This threat deals primarily with fraud and abuse. Fraud involves outright theft by employees who purchase items—for example, a wristwatch—to use exclusively for their own personal use. Abuse occurs when employes take advantage of their authority. For example, an employee authorized to take someone to lunch for business purposes may include a family member or friend or may go to unnecessarily expensive restaurants.

4. Failing to Take Advantage of Discounts, Price Breaks, or Discount Periods   The variance in purchasing price for a single product can be significant. While uncommon, it is possible to pay twice as much for a product from one vendor at one point in time as for the same product from another vendor at a different point in time. While there are advantages to buying from friends, customers of the business, and so forth, the purchasing function is a business within a business. This function accounts for a large percentage of the expenditure of business funds and should be properly managed. Failure to take advantage of discounts, price breaks, or discount periods can cause the cost of purchased items to increase significantly.

5. Purchasing Too Much or Unneeded Products   A frequently overlooked threat is the situation in which purchases are properly authorized, purchased at the lowest price and for the best quality, and then the product is not needed. It is a heartbreaking task for many owners to throw away unneeded inventory or to sell it at less than cost. Businesses may salvage some of their purchase price through deep discounting or selling inventory for scrap, but they certainly can't make a profit doing so. In an ideal situation, the day the very last item is sold, the product is either restocked in inventory or not restocked because demand has disappeared. While the ideal is not normally feasible, close attention must be paid to the need for items purchased.

CONTROL RULE OF THUMB 16

Never feel pleased about the money received for inventory sold as scrap. It doesn't take many brains to sell dollar bills for twenty five cents.

HOW SHOULD I STRUCTURE MY STAFF?

The owner or manager of a small business should take responsibility for initiating all major purchases. Good purchasing policy states that different approval levels are needed for purchases of different amounts. In addition, certain types of purchases, particularly nonrecurring ones such as the purchase of office equipment, should be either authorized by or under the direct control of the owner or manager of the business.

Unless there are large numbers of purchases, it is advisable to have a member of management approve each purchase. The approved purchase order becomes a necessary ingredient before an item can be paid for. This simple control ensures that the authorization process is followed.

There are three distinct functions in the purchasing-and-payables activity that should be separated among three people wherever possible. Although it is recognized that the individuals will probably work very closely together, control is improved when the functions are segregated. Note that none of these jobs has to be a full-time job, just a full-time responsibility.

The three purchasing-and-payables areas that should be divided are:

1. Initiating the Purchase   One individual should be assigned accountability for purchasing. In very small businesses this might be the owner or manager, while in larger businesses it may become a full-time function. As purchases grow in dollar amounts, a trained purchasing agent may be able to save enough money to pay his or her salary and still return a sizable investment to the business. Note that this individual is not the one initiating requirements but merely the one who develops the order and makes arrangements with vendors to acquire products. This function should include competitive bidding and maintaining records on vendor prices, discount periods, and price breaks.

2. Receiving Products   All merchandise purchased by the organization should be received by one person at a centralized point. In other words, items should not be delivered directly to the person ordering the product but, rather, sent to a central receiving point. where the receipt should be logged, the condition and quantity noted, and the product then delivered to the appropriate individual. This does not have to be a complex process. The purchasing agent gives one copy of the purchase order to the individual responsible for receiving. When items come in, the receiving person locates the appropriate copy of the purchase order and makes the necessary notations. He or she then delivers the product to the appropriate individual and gives the notated purchase order to the person in charge of paying for the purchase.

3. Payment for Purchases   The individual paying for purchases should be separate from the person ordering products and the person receiving products. The purchasing individual should send one copy of the purchase order to the payment clerk. The receiving person also sends a copy to the payment clerk. The clerk matches the two, and that becomes the basis for payment. The payment clerk should note whether payment is to be made from invoice, from shipping memo accompanied with the receipt of goods, or from statement mailed by the vendor.

Copies of the purchase order should be filed according to the date when payment is due. The payment clerk should be responsible for making all payments within the discount period. Missing a discount is a very expensive way of obtaining funds for short-term use.

If no discount is granted for early payment, then payables should be paid as late as possible. Payment can be made on the last possible date granted by the vendor or on the closest specified payment date of the business. Many businesses pay their bills twice a month, for example, on the first and fifteenth.

WHAT ARE THE KEY CONTROLS?

A category of controls used by many businesses is called "anticipation controls." This means that controls are established to anticipate some unfavorable or noteworthy event before it occurs. Good purchasing systems take advantage of these anticipation controls. For example, items of inventory have predetermined reorder points. When a particular item of stock falls below a quantity of, say, fifteen on hand, the product is reordered. This is an anticipation control to avoid running out of stock of that particular item.

The key controls in the purchasing-and-payables activity are:

1. Formal Purchase Order   Creating a request to purchase product using a formal purchase order fulfills the following control objectives:

• It documents the purchase process.
• It provides a document for management approval.
• It establishes a means to verify the correctness of vendor invoices.
• It helps prevent unauthorized purchases.
• It lessens the probability of acquiring wrong products from the vendor (because the vendor gets a copy of the purchase order).

The purchase order, together with any vendor invoice or shipping memo, can be used to record the products received. (The handling of inventories will be covered in Chapter 7.) If the item purchased is property, plant, or equipment, it is a depreciable asset and should be recorded on the books of the corporation as a depreciable asset. This includes a description of the property, cost of the property, expected life of the property, and the method of depreciation, such as accelerated or straight line.

It is advisable to have purchase orders prenumbered. This helps in controlling paperwork, as missing purchase orders can be easily detected. Note that most of the forms referred to in this book can be obtained from any office supply store.

2. Formal Receiving Process   One or more individuals should be assigned the responsibility of accepting products when delivered to the business. Ideally this person or persons would not be directly associated with control over inventory, purchasing, or payables. The receiving function entails the following tasks:

- Counting and examining the products received
- Signing with the shipper or vendor for the product
- Determining that the product was ordered (normally through a file copy of the purchase order)
- Noting quantities received and sending that notification to the payables clerk for payment
- Sending the product to the individual who ordered the product

3. Matching Purchase to Receiving Document Prior to Payment   The quantity and product on the purchase order should be matched to the product and quantity received as noted on the receiving report. In many instances these will be two copies of the purchase document. One copy can be used to record the quantity and product received. The accounts payable clerk then takes the receiving document and matches it to the invoice prior to paying the invoice.

4. Open Bidding   In many cases the business will not know the lowest price available for a product. One way to obtain this information is to permit multiple vendors to bid on the same order. The vendors selected for bidding can come from any of the following sources:

- Telephone yellow pages
- Trade associations and chambers of commerce

- Business colleagues and friends
- Competitors and trade associations
- Open advertising in newspapers and trade journals

Many businesses eventually find what they believe to be the low bidder. When this occurs, it is not unreasonable to purchase product from that vendor over a period of time. However, to ensure that that vendor keeps providing you the lowest price, tell the vendor that from time to time you will be going out for low bids, and then periodically do just that.

5. Independent Bank Reconciliation and Scrutiny of Checks The checking account should be reconciled by someone other than the individual who writes the checks, ideally by a member of senior business management. At the time the bank account is reconciled, scrutinize the checks for unusual payees and/or amounts. Also examine endorsements, and, where unusual, undertake additional investigation. For example, a check endorsed by an employee or endorsed by many people might cause suspicion.

6. Formal Payment Process The rules associated with paying bills should be formalized. The types of rules that are effective in reducing losses are to:

- Pay all bills by prenumbered checks bearing the company name.
- Use a mechanical check protector.
- Require the owner's or manager's signature on all checks.
- Never allow presigning of checks.
- Keep blank checks locked up. Blank checks also should be prenumbered.
- Discourage personal delivery of checks or cash by employees to creditors.
- Not make checks payable to "bearer" or to "cash" except under special circumstances.
- Require the owner's or manager's approval of document.
- Note on bill (invoice) that it has been paid.
- Retain an account for all voided checks.
- Follow up on checks that remain outstanding over sixty days.

7. Purchasing Planning   Periodically the business should do detailed planning on the type, quantity, and delivery schedule for needed
products. The plan should take into account business fluctuations in
sales, as well as opportunities to purchase products in either economic
quantities or at special discount times. This type of planning should
allow the business to enter into long-term purchase contracts that may
offer more desirable prices than unplanned periodic purchases.

8. No Company Charge Cards   It is frequently advisable for
employees to have charge cards. For example, sales and management
personnel may be required to travel for the business, to entertain, and
so forth. Having a charge card ensures that that individual will have the
appropriate cash. However, if it is a company charge card, the company is responsible for the bills and the invoices are sent directly to the
company. It is far superior to have the card be in the name of the
employee and have the employee submit the expenses on an expense
statement for reimbursement by the company. If there is a charge for the
card, that should be a reimbursable expense. If the employee ter-
minates, or plans to terminate, or just plain abuses the credit card
privilege, the charges will then go to that employee personally and not
to the company.

WHAT THREATS DO THE KEY
CONTROLS ADDRESS?

The purchasing-and-payables activity threats addressed by the
previously described key controls are illustrated in Figure 6-1. This
matrix shows which controls are effective against which threats.
Managers should use this matrix in selecting and installing specific controls.

IF I CAN ONLY AFFORD TWO CONTROLS,
WHAT SHOULD THEY BE?

One of the most important functions that management can perform to
control purchasing is planning. It is through good planning that the
needed inventory and support products will be matched with the
demands of the corporation. However, while essential, this is not listed

Key Controls \ Threats	Paying for Product Not Received	Paying Twice for Product	Purchasing Unauthorized Product	Failing to Take Advantage of Discounts, Price Breaks, or Discount Period	Purchasing Too Much or Unneeded Product
Formal purchase order			✔		
Formal receiving process	✔				
Matching purchase to receiving document prior to payment	✔	✔			
Open bidding				✔	
Independent bank reconciliation and scrutiny of checks			✔		
Formal payment process	✔	✔	✔	✔	
Purchasing planning				✔	✔
No company charge cards	✔		✔		

Figure 6-1 PURCHASING-AND-PAYABLES THREAT-REDUCTION MATRIX

as one of the two key controls because it does not address the problems of loss, abuse, and theft.

If only two key purchasing-and-payables controls could be implemented due to cost constraints, the recommended two are:

1. *Matching purchase to receiving document prior to payment.* This step provides reasonable assurance that the items being paid for have been received. In addition, if the matching is done by someone

in a responsible position, the documents can be scrutinized for need. While this scrutiny may not allow the business to avoid paying the invoice in hand, it may lead to some changes in the purchasing practice to reduce future losses.

2. *Having a formal payment process.* Much of the business resources will be passed through the payables system. It is essential that some basic controls be installed over the cash disbursement process. The formalization of this process, which involves eliminating potential vulnerabilities such as signing blank checks, will provide management greater assurance that the funds are being used for needed purposes.

HOW DO I KNOW THE CONTROLS WORK?

Management needs to scrutinize continually the effectiveness of the purchasing policy of the business. Such attention is not only useful for control purposes but should provide some valuable input into the purchasing planning process. The assessment of the purchasing-and-payables activities involves verifying the reasonableness of the financial account balances and assessing the adequacy of the activity controls.

Substantive Tests

Purchasing and payables are both items associated with the income and expense statement. Checking the financial balance of one of these accounts is not like verifying cash in the bank. Purchasing is the cumulative account of the total purchases over the year. Therefore, the substantiation of that figure will be more dependent on the adequacy of controls than on substantive-type tests that might be performed. However, the substantive tests do help evaluate the reasonableness of the total disbursements through the payables function.

The tests that can be performed to substantiate the purchasing-and-payables activity are:

1. Gross Profit Test The same test that was used to substantiate the reasonableness of sales will also substantiate purchasing. This is a relational test that is one of the stronger tests in substantiating the reasonableness of financial figures.

2. Product Scrutiny Management should periodically tour the plant and office to assess the condition and quantity of products on hand. The objective of this test is to evaluate the reasonableness of the types and quantities of purchases. In doing this, the manager should be on the particular lookout for:

- Items that appear overstocked
- Products that are growing "dust"
- Damaged goods
- Products whose cartons or covers are turning color with age
- Products stored in hard-to-reach locations

Products in any of these conditions warrant further investigation. The apparently unneeded products may not pose a serious problem in and of themselves, but could if still being ordered.

3. Ratio Test The cost of sales should remain relatively constant from period to period. For example, if the cost of sales is averaging 67 percent of sales, then one might expect that number not to fluctuate too much over a period of time. If it does fluctuate significantly upward or downward, this should be of concern to management. The fluctuation may be bad or good; it may represent a theft or improved performance. What is important from a managerial control perspective is that the variance be noted, investigated, and the cause determined.

The amount of products purchased should relate directly to the sales. However, because of volume purchasing, special sales, or other reasons for inconsistent purchasing, that percentage may vary significantly during shorter periods. For example, it might be 50 percent one month and 70 percent the next. However, over an extended period of time, usually six months or one year, the ratios should remain fairly common. They are good indicators of problems if there is a significant variation.

CONTROL RULE OF THUMB 17

Managerial scrutiny and instinct are some of the strongest controls for detecting problems in a small business.

Internal Control Self-Assessment Checklist

Checklist 3 is designed to provide a self-assessment on the adequacy of controls over the purchasing-and-payables activity. *Yes* answers are indicative of good control practices, and *no* answers are indicative of potential control vulnerabilities. *No* answers should be investigated to determine whether or not controls should be strengthened.

Checklist 3   PURCHASING-AND-PAYABLES SELF-ASSESSMENT

	Response			
Item	*Yes*	*No*	*N/A*	*Comments*
1. Is a requisition procedure required before making purchases?				
2. Have guidelines been established for vendor acceptability, such as past performance, reputation and credit standing, ability to meet delivery, quality and service specifications, price competitiveness, and policies on related party transactions?				
3. Has an approved-vendor list been prepared based on the above guidelines?				
4. Do the purchase orders contain an agreed-on price or an expected price?				
5. Is it mandatory that purchase orders be approved by someone in a responsible position other than the one creating the purchase order?				
6. Has a policy been established for returning unacceptable items to vendors for credit?				
7. Are receiving reports prepared for all items received? (This may simply involve making indications on a copy of the purchase order.)				
8. Are purchase orders and receiving documents matched before payment is made?				

Checklist 3 PURCHASING-AND-PAYABLES SELF-ASSESSMENT (Continued)

		Response		
Item	Yes	No	N/A	Comments
9. Are vendor discounts taken?				
10. Is the accounts payable subsidiary ledger regularly reconciled with the general ledger account?				
11. Are all invoices canceled after payment?				
12. Are all received items counted?				
13. Is there segregation of duties between the accounts payable and cash disbursements functions?				
14. Are checks prenumbered and all checks accounted for?				
15. Have safekeeping procedures been established for blank checks and facsimile signature plates?				
16. Are the terms of purchase clearly stated on purchase orders?				
17. Are rates charged by common carriers verified prior to payment?				

7

controlling inventory

Inventory may be the single greatest asset of the business. The more highly marketable the inventory, the more vulnerable the business to loss and theft. If the business sells high-fashion merchandise, food, small appliances, or other high-demand consumer products, the temptation to steal will be greater than for some commercial products. The control over inventory must address the threat concern, as well as the proper storage and retention of inventory.

This chapter reviews how to control the inventory activity. The major inventory threats are identified, and the controls effective in reducing those threats are discussed. The chapter provides a series of tests that a manager can perform to evaluate the right inventory is on hand and to evaluate the adequacy of inventory controls.

WHAT IS THE MANAGEMENT
INVENTORY CHALLENGE?

The impact of employee theft on small businesses is larger than most business people realize. The facts and figures presented by the Small Business Bureau are frequently staggering. Because inventory is one of the more vulnerable assets, it is important to have good inventory controls.

Detecting small theft losses through the accounting records is virtually impossible. Therefore, it is better to strive for prevention rather than after-the-fact detection of loss. Good basic controls such as making it difficult to have physical access to inventory and then barring unauthorized people from the inventory area proves very helpful in reducing loss.

Businesses should maintain good records on their inventory. These records need to indicate the amount of stock on hand, quantities set aside for specific customers, and items that are on consignment. Good inventory control is essential to the successful operations of most businesses.

In fulfilling the business inventory requirements, management has the following challenges:

1. Safeguarding Inventory It is necessary in many businesses to put inventory on display, as, for example, in retailing and food stores. This makes inventory especially vulnerable. Inventory used in the office and for administrative purposes has value to employees for their personal business. Employees, customers, and service people moving in and out of the business premises are tempted to grab handfuls of inventory to take it with them.

Items of equipment, office machines, and furnishings are also candidates for theft, particularly small office machines and computers. A common technique for removing small office equipment is to put the item in a bag of trash; before the trash collector comes to pick it up, the employee collects the item from the outside trash storage area.

Inventory losses can mean the difference between a profitable and unprofitable year for some businesses. In addition, inventory can be damaged, which can be just as costly to the business as theft. Management must attempt to store and secure inventory in such a manner that losses are minimized.

2. Minimizing Stockouts A *stockout* occurs when there is insufficient inventory to meet customer demand. In many cases this will result in a lost sale, even if inventory can be replenished quickly.

The following three techniques are used to minimize stockouts:

- Maintain perpetual inventory records.
- Predetermine reorder points.
- Predetermine economic order quantities.

When these three conditions are present, adequate records will be maintained; when the reorder point is reached, the predetermined economic order quantity can be purchased.

3. Identifying a Sufficient Source of Supply Management should maintain records on multiple sources for key inventory, supplies, or both. If a regular vendor should be out of a needed product, management should have alternate sources to call on. For this reason, many businesses maintain accounts with two or more suppliers of needed products. Should one supplier be short of a product, then the business, who is also a regular customer of another supplier, has a good opportunity of acquiring the needed product from that second supplier. The challenge of inventory is associated with the challenges of purchasing and cash management. The purchasing system has the challenge of acquiring the needed inventory. However, the purchasing system may be restricted by cash-flow problems. Therefore, the total inventory planning process includes inventory management, cash management, and purchasing.

WHY SHOULD I BE CONCERNED?
(THE THREATS)

Previously I described the two variables of threat as frequency of occurrence and loss per occurrence; control emphasis should be placed on whichever variable is greater in a given situation. In the case of inventory the greater variable may be dependent on the value of the inventory.

Low-priced inventory normally puts the control emphasis on frequency of occurrence. For example, in a food market most items are of low value, so the store is concerned about the volume of items stolen rather than which items are stolen. On the other hand, as the value of inventory increases, the controls shift from the frequency variable to the loss variable in the formula. Because each item takes on importance, the controls center around securing each item. For example, in a jewelry store, controls are directed at locking up all of the valuable jewelry.

The specific threats are:

1. Inventory Damaged Poor inventory handling or poor inventory storage conditions can result in damaged products. In addition, some products may be damaged by change in humidity and temperature, as well as wind or rain damage. The types and methods of storage should be consistent with the proper protection of the inventory.

Well-laid-out warehouses with good moving equipment tend to minimize damage. Organizations that use public warehouses should look for the same type of conditions in those warehouses they demand in their own business locations. Most losses are preventable by good controls.

2. Inventory Missing   Inventory can be missing because it has been stored in the wrong location, accidently discarded, or shipped in error to a customer or other location. (Theft is another reason inventory might be missing, but that is not included within this category.) Even small organizations are frequently unable to find inventory they believe to have on hand. In these instances the business may have to buy additional inventory, when in fact that inventory is located somewhere on the premises.

3. Inventory Theft   In most businesses, theft of inventory is the greatest theft threat. In some retail organizations, theft accounts for over 5 percent of the inventory usage. These losses must be reflected in higher prices to the customers, which may have a negative impact on sales if other similar businesses are able to keep theft at a lower level.

If the ingenuity used by employees in stealing inventory could be channeled into profitable directions, businesses would significantly increase their profits. Some of the more common ways of removing inventory are:

- After-hour requisitions by employees
- Carrying items off the premises in lunch pails, briefcases, and pocketbooks and under garments
- Mailing or shipping inventory to friends
- Discarding items as "trash"
- Sending items out with incoming delivery people

CONTROL RULE OF THUMB 18
In designing controls, if there is ever a choice between the concerns of incompetence and greed, experience has shown that incompetence will cause the greater loss.

4. Out-of-Stock Condition Out-of-stock conditions occur because of:

• Unanticipated demand
• Improper perpetual inventory records
• Poor planning
• Vendors also being out of stock

5. Inventory Improperly Identified Large losses can occur due to shipping the wrong product, shipping current rather than older stocks, or assuming an out-of-stock condition exists when inventory is actually within the warehouse. These losses are associated with not being able either to identify the specific item of inventory sold or to decide which items should be sold first. Also when many wrong items are shipped (because they are not properly identified) the cost of returning those items can be large.

6. Inventory Overvalued Obsolete or excessive inventory may be worth less than the value as recorded on the books of the business. As a result, the value and the profits of the business are overstated. For example, if the total book value of obsolete inventory were $10,000 but the inventory were only worth $2,000, then both the profit for the period and the value of the inventory on the corporation's books would be overstated by $8,000 (that is, $10,000 book value minus $2,000 real value equals $8,000 overstatement). Generally accepted accounting principles and tax laws permit the writedown of inventory to its true market value.

HOW SHOULD I STRUCTURE MY STAFF?

The management of inventory is an important function to a small business. In all but the smallest organizations one or more people will be required to store and distribute the inventory. I previously stated that receiving should be a separate function. In some businesses, receiving is combined with inventory storage. While not ideal, it is not unacceptable from a control perspective to have the inventory clerk also do the receiving.

There are two basic functions in inventory, which are best performed by separate individuals, as follows:

- *Inventory storage and retrieval.* One individual should be responsible for placing inventory in and retrieving inventory from the storage area. The purchasing system has the responsibility for acquiring additional inventory. This is shipped by vendors and then stored in the inventory area. As the inventory is needed, it is withdrawn. In larger organizations withdrawal should be formalized and authorized. In smaller businesses withdrawal may be less formal but still should be recorded. The individual maintaining the inventory should also keep perpetual records on stock in inventory. In some businesses this is performed by computer. When manually prepared, the process need only involve a card maintained next to each item or a centrally located ledger that contains a running on-hand balance of each item.

- *Distribution of goods to customers.* Distributing inventory to customers should be handled by someone other than the person maintaining the inventory records. In some businesses, inventory is packed and shipped to customers. If the individual maintaining the records has the opportunity to ship product outside the business premises, unauthorized shipments could be made using the same means. Good control practices allow the person maintaining the inventory to pull it from the shelves and get it ready for shipment. At that point a second person checks the quantity against the customer's purchase order to determine that it is correct. This double check not only reduces theft but helps eliminate the inventory error of shipping the wrong product.

In retail establishments, one individual replenishes the inventory in the store while another sells and distributes it to customers.

WHAT ARE THE KEY CONTROLS?

Controls are any measure, means, or procedure used by management to reduce losses. Unfortunately, control frequently has a negative connotation. If management appears to have too many controls, employees may feel they are not being trusted or are too limited in their abilities to take action. Therefore it is suggested that management not continue to talk in terms of controls but, rather, use the word *procedures*. To most individuals, except the control purists, a procedure is just a preferred way of doing something while a control is a constraint placed on an individual by management. If employees are happier with procedures than controls, call the concepts in this book procedures.

The key controls that have proved effective in the inventory activity are:

1. Perpetual Inventory Records   A *perpetual inventory* is a running record of the amount of inventory on hand. The exactness of the records should be consistent with the needs of the inventory records. For example, in some businesses products can be stored so that counting the products is easy. In this instance the perpetual inventory records may involve stacking the product a certain way, as opposed to writing numbers on a piece of paper.

2. Secure Storage Area   The protection provided the inventory should be consistent with the value of the inventory. At a minimum, inventory should be stored in a remote area not readily accessible to customers, vendors, service people, and so on. Obviously, this doesn't apply to the inventory on display but to the inventory in a storage area. As the value of the inventory increases, the security measures should also increase. Some of the physical security measures include:

• Bars on windows and doors
• Surveillance devices
• Security protection by police, private detective agencies, security guards, and so forth
• Guard dogs

3. Alarm Tags   Many retailers secure special tags to the merchandise kept on their premises. This is most frequently done with garments. The exits to the store have alarms that are triggered if the merchandise is carried through the door with the tag still attached. When a customer buys the product, the store removes the tag with a special tool. Without the use of this tool the customer would have to destroy the garment to get the tag off and remove the garment from the premises. Bookstores also are using this control to prevent books from being stolen.

4. Storage Bins, Racks, Pallets, and So On   Good storage practices result in minimal damaged goods. The use of proper facilities also significantly increases the amount of storage that can be placed into a small area. Businesses that feel they lack sufficient storage space may wish to engage the services of a warehouse consultant to help them lay out their storage area. Some of these consultants work for the companies that sell storage racks and provide that service at no extra cost.

5. Reorder Points   This control involves predetermining the point at which inventory should be reordered. Some of the reorder considerations include:

- Average volume of sales
- Length of time to receive the next order
- Storage material available
- Cost of inventory

6. Requisition Form   This is a form that must be used before inventory is removed from the storage area. Very small organizations may not want to formalize the withdrawal process, but in larger organizations this may be a cost-effective control. At a minimum, records should be maintained on who removes inventory from storage and how much is removed.

7. Inventory Tags   An inventory tag is an easy-to-read sign or marker indicating which product is stored in which area. If the product is self-identifying, inventory tags are normally not necessary. However, if it is difficult to differentiate two or more products, or the products do not contain an indication of what they are, then inventory tags are extremely helpful.

8. Writeoff or Scrap   Periodically, items carried in inventory should be grouped according to their status as obsolete, excessive, or good. Such a procedure calls attention to declines in the inventory's value. Promptly writing off excess and obsolete inventory prevents overstatement and gives the owner or manager a more realistic picture of the company's value. In reviewing these writeoffs, the business should indicate what it considers about its past performance in estimating purchases and sales and should act accordingly.

WHAT THREATS DO THE KEY CONTROLS ADDRESS?

The ability to select the right control for the right circumstance is not yet a science. There is no magic formula that a business can use to say that in any given situation such-and-such is the "best" control. The threat-reduction matrices provided in this book are an attempt to help businesses select the right control. However, you should be warned that these concepts are not foolproof and judgment should still be used.

The key controls that are effective in reducing the inventory threats are shown in Figure 7-1. Note that in many instances more than one control can be used to reduce a specific threat. If the person selecting the control is unsure which one to use, the following guidelines may prove helpful:

Threats / Key Controls	Inventory Damaged	Inventory Missing	Inventory Stolen	Out-of-Stock Condition	Improperly Identified	Inventory Overvalued
Perpetual inventory records		✔	✔	✔		
Secure storage area		✔	✔			
Alarms tags			✔			
Storage bins, racks, pallets, and so on	✔				✔	
Reorder points				✔		
Requisition form	✔	✔				
Inventory tags					✔	
Writeoff or scrap						✔

Figure 7-1 INVENTORY THREAT-REDUCTION MATRIX

1. If two or more threats are of concern, select the control that addresses as many of the threats of concern as possible.
2. Select the control that is indicated as one of the two key controls discussed in the following section.
3. Select the control that is most understandable and easiest to install.

IF I CAN ONLY AFFORD TWO CONTROLS, WHAT SHOULD THEY BE?

Inventory is the lifeblood of most businesses. If customers do not have the right inventory, in the right condition, and at the right time, they may flock to their competitors. Therefore, while theft is a very large concern in inventory, the two key controls selected are more important for survival than for reducing theft. The two recommended controls in the inventory activity are:

1. Perpetual inventory records - Without good records, businesses will not know when to reorder. When they do not reorder at the appropriate time, they will get out of stock. Too many stockouts invariably results in a loss of business because customers will go to the business with the inventory on hand.
2. Storage bins, racks, pallets, and so on - The efficiency and productivity of the business may be dependent on the ease with which the business can get needed inventory. In addition, well-laid-out storage rooms help keep product in good condition. While a well-laid-out storage area may not reduce theft, it does make scrutiny by management easier and may make theft more noticeable, which helps deter theft.

HOW DO I KNOW THE CONTROLS WORK?

Control is not a guarantee of zero losses. Losses are not eliminated with control, nor are they guaranteed without control. Control is designed to reduce the probability of losses. As such, the assessment of the adequacy of control will not be an exact science but rather a judgment. However, without that judgment, imprecise as it may be, management may be sustaining losses it is unaware of or may be wasting control dollars.

Inventory controls are assessed in two ways: first, by testing the correctness of the on-hand inventory; and second, by evaluating the adequacy of controls that protect that inventory.

Substantive Tests

Management can test the adequacy of the inventory balance by using one of the following methods:

1. *Unannounced spot check*. Periodically on an unannounced basis, management should count one or more items of inventory. The manager should obtain the perpetual inventory record amount, adjust that by any inventory held on consignment or for customers, and then verify that the actual on-hand balance is in agreement with the perpetual inventory amount. If there are differences, these should be investigated.

2. *Conduct a physical inventory*. At least once per year a complete physical inventory should be conducted. The general guidelines that make a physical inventory successful are to:

   - Conduct the physical inventory during nonworking hours.
   - Have the physical inventory made by people other than those directly responsible for inventory.
   - Have all like inventory placed together in a single location for the count.
   - Have personnel knowledgeable with inventory ensure that all inventory is properly identified.
   - Develop count sheets so that the people conducting the counts can easily record them.
   - Have all inventory counted twice by two different people.
   - Reconcile perpetual and book inventory the day of the count.
   - Immediately investigate differences.
   - If there are significant differences, tighten inventory controls to prevent losses from occuring. In addition, physical inventory should be conducted more often than annually.

3. *Record and investigate customer inventory complaints.* Complaints by customers that they have been shipped the wrong product, the wrong quantity, or products they did not order warrant investigation. If theft of any size is occurring, there is the probability that some of the customers of the business will either receive those products in error or become alert because of other suspicious circumstances. To ignore these events may result in not identifying problems early.

4. *Wastebasket check.* Employees become involved in all sorts of capers. Many of the plans for fraud and abuse get committed to paper. Original documents are destroyed and new documents introduced. Some of the planning documents, old and new documents that are not needed, are thrown out in the trash. This becomes a haven of evidence about what is going on in the business. Some managers during nonworking hours periodically conduct wastebasket checks, which can also include desk or work station checks, as a means of uncovering improper events.

Internal Control Self-Assessment Checklist

Inventory controls are some of the more important controls in the business. The more valuable the inventory, the more the owner must rely on the inventory controls. Therefore the frequency of assessing the adequacy of inventory controls should be related to the value of the inventory. It may be advisable to assess these controls more than once per year.

Checklist 4 is designed to help the owner or manager assess the adequacy of the inventory controls. *Yes* answers are indicative of good control practices and *no* answers represent potential vulnerabilities. If the user of the checklist is uncertain of the significance of the vulnerability, discuss it with the business's accountant.

Checklist 4 INVENTORY SELF-ASSESSMENT

Item		*Response*			
		Yes	*No*	*N/A*	*Comments*
1. If products are manufactured, are bills of material developed for those goods being produced?					

Checklist 4 INVENTORY SELF-ASSESSMENT (Continued)

Item	Response			
	Yes	No	N/A	Comments
2. Are there policies for determining excess or obsolete inventory quantities?				
3. Has responsibility been assigned for review and approval of adjustments to inventory?				
4. Is there a requirement that all movements or shipments of merchandise and assets at a physical facility be accompanied by appropriate documentation?				
5. Is there a periodic follow-up on disposition of inventory identified as obsolete or excessive?				
6. Is a physical inventory of items on hand performed at least once per performed at least once per year?				
7. Are significant differences between physical and book inventory investigated?				
8. Are physical inventories of fixed assets conducted periodically?				
9. Are inventory pricing policies in conformity with generally accepted accounting procedures?				
10. Are appropriate identification tags attached to inventory and fixed assets on acquisition?				
11. Are back orders properly controlled?				
12. Is damaged, unordered, or unwanted merchandise returned?				

8

controlling cash

Almost all business transactions involve cash at some point. Therefore, controlling and protecting cash is one of the major control problems facing a business. The type and extent of internal control over cash depends on the availability of personnel, the skill of the people, the type of record keeping (manual or automated), the volume of transactions, the type of cash receipt (cash or check), and the method of receiving cash (direct from customers, through the mail, via courier, or by other methods).

Cash is an essential ingredient to the success of the business. A corporation that runs out of cash may be forced out of business or into bankruptcy. The management of cash to ensure the appropriate cash flow is equally as important as the controls over loss and misuse of cash.

This chapter describes management's cash responsibilities and the threats to those responsibilities. Controls that are effective for handling cash are described and then related to the specific threat they reduce. The chapter concludes with the types of tests and control assessments that management can make to ensure the proper handling of cash in the business.

WHAT IS THE MANAGEMENT'S
CASH-CONTROL CHALLENGE?

Management has two basic cash challenges. First, there must be enough cash available to pay the bills of the corporation, and second, management must prevent the theft and abuse of cash. In addressing these challenges, management has the following five cash-management responsibilities:

121

1. Receiving Cash Cash can arrive at a business in a variety of ways. The type of business and kinds of interactions with the customer frequently dictates the form in which cash is received. In some retail organizations it is primarily cash, while in others it is through charges paid by check. Both methods require control.

The timely recording of cash, regardless of method of receipt, is the strongest single cash control. For example, if cash is received, the cash registers, sales invoices, or log sheets can all be effective means if the employee immediately records the cash transaction.

Mail should always be opened in a controlled manner. In very small businesses the owner or manager should personally open the mail. In larger businesses there should be a minimum of two employees present when the mail is opened. Any cash or checks arriving in the mail should be recorded on a log sheet. The cash and checks should then be separated from the paperwork. Checks should immediately be endorsed with a restrictive endorsement stamp.

When cash is received, it is important to record the purpose for which that cash was received, such as payment of merchandise, payment of sales tax, shipping charges, payment of an accounts receivable, sale of fixed assets, and so on. As you can perceive, there are different liabilities and tax implications for different types of receipts. In the case of receivables it is important to know who paid the receivable.

In some cases there will be cash receipts for which the purpose is unknown. Many businesses receive cash in the mail with no identification other than a company name, checks from businesses that do not owe them money and for which the purpose is not stated. In some cases, extra cash appears that cannot be accounted for (note that it can also be missing), and sometimes personnel will forget to record from whom or why the cash was acquired. In these instances a *"suspense"* *file* should be maintained. This is a small log indicating date, amount of cash, who received it if appropriate, any identification known about the cash, and, when determined, who it was from and for what purpose. Someone in management should take follow-up action if sufficient information is available. If not, the log should be retained in the event that there is a customer inquiry regarding the resolution of an order or some other purpose for the cash payment.

2. Depositing Cash Cash should be deposited intact on a daily basis. At the end of each working day, all cash receipts should be bundled and deposited. During this process, a reconciliation sheet is normally prepared showing the source of all cash and perhaps some cash liabilities such as sales tax.

It is recommended that all cash receipts be deposited in a single bank account. This makes the cash accountability easier. If it is desirable to have separate bank accounts or investment accounts, funds can then be transferred from the primary account to the other accounts as desired.

3. Disbursing Cash   Cash must be disbursed in order to pay company bills, do payroll, transfer funds, and provide distribution of profits to the owners and stockholders of the business. All cash disbursements should be made by check. Checks should be signed by a responsible member of management or through the use of a check-signing machine under the control of a responsible individual.

It is good practice at the time of check signing to have the paperwork supporting the payment and the check together. This enables the individual signing the check to review the paperwork and evaluate the legitimacy and need for the disbursement.

Disbursements should be made by prenumbered checks and all checks should be accounted for. The company's name and the purpose of the payment should be included on the check where appropriate. For example, the purpose of routine payment of supplies, inventory, and payroll will be relatively obvious to the payee, but nonstandard payments such as the purchase of equipment should be noted on the check.

4. Accounting for Cash   Organizations must maintain adequate records on cash receipts and disbursements. The procedures described in the receiving, depositing, and disbursing responsibilities provide the basic source documents for cash accounting. The two basic records that an organization needs for cash accounting are a cash-receipts journal and a cash-disbursements journal.

These two journals may take a variety of forms. For example, the *cash-receipts journal* can be a cash register tape, a formal accounting journal in which cash receipts are listed, a computer system, a series of sales invoices, or a daily cash-receipts reconciliation form. A *cash-disbursements journal* can be a checkbook, a pegboard (a form of a checkbook in which the checks are overlaid on the cash disbursements journal so that in the process of writing the check the disbursement is posted in the journal), a computer, or a series of vouchers authorizing the payment of cash.

The size and complexity of the cash-receipts and -disbursements journals will depend on the volume of cash transactions. The system adopted should be no more complex than the business volume warrants. Generally, the simpler the system the better.

CONTROL RULE OF THUMB 19

Pay your accountant to set up your company's accounting records. It is money well invested.

---

5. Investing Cash   Idle cash is a wasted resource. Money has a value. Interest or other investment income can contribute to the profit of the business.

Business management must manage cash in the same manner that it manages employees and inventory. Managing cash involves understanding investment options, cash-flow projections, revenue and expenditure planning based on expected income and expenses, and the selection of appropriate investments for the business.

Corporations have basically all of the cash investment options open to individuals, including:

- Interest-bearing accounts in banks and certificates of deposit
- Purchase of stocks and bonds
- Investment in real estate
- Tax shelters

   Note that certain corporate investments in stocks and bonds generate income that is not subject to federal corporate income tax.

CONTROL RULE OF THUMB 20

Income earned on the investment of cash is a 100 percent contribution to bottom-line profit.

WHY SHOULD I BE CONCERNED?
(THE THREATS)

The money management threats address the challenges of inadequate funds to pay bills and the loss of cash. The specific threats that should be of concern to management are:

1. Inadequate Cash Flow   Current and future business decisions all depend on the cash flow of the business. The availability or nonavailability of cash is a major concern of management when deciding what levels of inventory are to be established, how many employees are needed, what salaries can be paid to management, and what type of expansions the business can engage in.

Cash-flow projections can only be developed when management has done income and expense planning (discussed in Chapter 10). If management prepares a budgeted income statement, the cash-flow projection can be easily developed from that budget.

Cash flow is normally determined on a monthly basis. It begins with the current cash balance. For each month the cash income items included in the budget are added to the on-hand cash balance. These items include expected cash receipts, payment on receivables, interest income, and so forth. Projected cash outlays are then subtracted from this balance. These include planned payments to vendors, employee salaries, tax payments, and any distribution of profit to the owners or shareholders. This will then show a projected cash balance at the end of the cash-flow planning period.

Once these cash-flow projections are developed, management must realize that since the cash-flow projection is based on budgeted income, any variation will directly affect cash flow. For example, the cash-flow projection will need to be adjusted by any over- or undercollection of receivables and over- or underpayment of liabilities.

The small business that does not have a large reserve of cash must be sensitive to these variations. If it is a period in which the business is very short on cash, the cash-flow projections and adjustments may have to be done more often than monthly. When variations to budgeted income and expenses change, the cash-management program will have to be adjusted accordingly.

It is advisable for small businesses in tight cash-flow positions to arrange with a bank for *open credit*. If the business runs short of cash it has authorization in advance from the bank to borrow up to a predetermined amount. This can normally be arranged if the business has sufficient assets or reputation to provide security for such a line of credit.

2. Loss of Interest   If large amounts of cash are not invested, the manager runs the risk of loss of interest income. If the cash is left on the firm's premises, the manager runs additional risks of theft and destruction of cash. Only enough cash should be kept on the business premises to run the business for a day or a weekend.

The manager can determine the estimated sales for a particular day and keep a certain percentage of those sales on hand, which can be used for change and early sales returns. To keep cash at a minimum, additional bank deposits can be made during the day if sales are very heavy.

The cash in the bank should not be kept in a noninterest-bearing account. As soon as the minimum bank balance is achieved to offset service charges, the excess funds should be immediately moved to an interest-bearing account or other investment. If the amounts of cash are large, it is normally advisable to move cash daily between accounts. Some banks will do this automatically if the business requests it.

The proper investment of cash can be one of the major contributors to profitability. You must remember that insurance companies make almost all of their profit on cash investment and little or none from their insurance business. This is a good lesson to keep in mind when one begins to feel pride in a large balance in a noninterest-bearing account.

3. Loss of Cash   Uncontrolled cash is subject to the risk of loss. The loss can be due to theft, mismanagement, or destruction. While rare, fires have consumed large amounts of cash stored in businesses because the owner was too lazy to deposit it in the bank. Also, large amounts of cash tempt people to "borrow" a little for a day or two.

4. Inadequate Accounting   Cash that cannot be properly accounted for may be lost. One of the easiest ways to embezzle a business is to take the cash and alter the cash accounting accordingly. For example, if a customer pays in cash and there is no accounting of that cash, then the employee can take it without detection. On the other hand, if there is properly accounted for cash, for example, cash register ringing, then the theft of cash would be noticed. The principles to be followed in record keeping and accounting for cash are described in the chapter on controlling record keeping (Chapter 11).

HOW SHOULD I STRUCTURE MY STAFF?

In a very small business the owner or manager will be required to play a major role in cash management. In many instances that individual will perform many of the cash functions. As the business grows, there are three distinct cash-management functions, and these should be divided among three people. These are:

1. Receipt of Cash   The receipt of cash should be performed by an individual who has no other cash responsibilities. Responsibility of this individual will be to gather all the cash that has come into a business during the day or perhaps several times a day. The funds will be appropriately recorded on a cash reconciliation document or a bank deposit slip. This individual may also be responsible for depositing the cash in the bank. Previously it was suggested that the individual making the sale (Chapter 4) or opening the envelope (Chapter 5) be a different person from the one who actually got the cash for accumulating and depositing.

2. Cash Disbursements   The individual disbursing the cash should not have responsibility for cash receipts. Determining what cash is to be spent should be done by someone other than the individual making the disbursement, unless he or she happens to be the owner or manager of the business.

3. Accounting for Cash   The accounting function should be performed by someone who is responsible for neither receipts nor disbursements. In smaller businesses where this is not practical, it may be advisable to have the closing of the books done by the business's accountant. In addition, the bank account should be reconciled by someone not having cash responsibilities. In many instances this will be the owner or manager of the business.

CONTROL RULE OF THUMB 21

No employee should be in a position to both "steal and conceal"—that is, take cash or inventory and then adjusting the books so that the theft would not be uncovered by the accounting system.

WHAT ARE THE KEY CONTROLS?

There are three basic elements of a control. These are (1) the method of implementation, (2) the purpose, and (3) the point at which it is implemented. All three aspects of a control are important.

The effectiveness of the control will vary based on how these three elements are applied. In many businesses the improper selection or application of a control has a net result of no control.

Let's look at an example of how an apparently good control may in effect be no control. Many businesses require two signatures on a check. The method is good because it involves two people, and the objective is good because it is attempting to eliminate unauthorized payments. The question in this instance is third control element, the point at which the control is applied. The control is applied to the check-signing and not the check-authorization process. The check may be made out to an authorized company for the correct amount but contains items purchased for the pleasure of employees. This would not be known in the check-signing process. However, it could be known in the check-authorization process. Thus, to achieve the appropriate objective, it is important to address the point in the system where the threat is the greatest.

CONTROL RULE OF THUMB 22
The control should be applied at the point in the system where the threat is the greatest.

A description follows of the controls effective in reducing money-management threats. The point at which the controls should be applied is listed in the money-management threat-prevention matrix (Figure 8-1) presented later in this chapter.

1. Cash Planning Cash planning is an activity involving the anticipation of and preparation for cash needs. The plan must identify the sources and timing of revenue, the purposes and timing of expenditure, the need for borrowing and investment, and any cash distribution to the owner.

Key Controls \ Threats	Inadequate Cash Flow	Loss of Interest	Loss of Cash	Inadequate Accounting
Cash planning	✓			
Short-term investment policy		✓		
Cash deposited intact			✓	
All disbursements made by check				✓
Limited-use petty cash fund				✓
Restrictive endorsement			✓	
Cash-receipts procedure			✓	✓
Bill-paying procedure			✓	✓
Independent bank-statement reconciliation			✓	

Figure 8-1 MONEY MANAGEMENT THREAT-REDUCTION MATRIX

2. Short-Term Investment Policy The method of investing excessive cash should be predetermined. This does not mean that the exact investment will always be decided but, rather, that a short-term cash investment policy will be established. In most businesses this involves the use of interest-bearing accounts, money market funds, or certificates of deposit. Long-term investments should be covered under cash planning, as they will change with cash availability. Someone in the business should then be accountable for implementing the short-term investment policy as excessive cash becomes available.

3. Cash Deposited Intact Monies collected should be bundled and deposited in the bank the same day the cash is received. It is generally good to make the deposits at the same time each day by the same person. Two deposit slips should be prepared, one retained in the business and one for deposit in the bank and is normally returned with the bank statement.

4. All Disbursements Made by Check   Checks provide a record of payment and provide a means of controlling that payment because it requires an authorized signature.

5. Limited-Use Petty Cash Fund   Even in a very small business, the owner cannot be expected to exercise complete authority in every transaction. There are times when some authority must be delegated to an employee. In the cash-disbursement area this can be accomplished through a petty cash fund. The fund should be established by check and then reimbursed by check based on the presentation of receipts for expenditures. The fund should be reserved for those situations that cannot easily be handled by check or that may occur when the manager is not present, such as paying postage due on mail. The funds should be kept small, usually about $100, and the purposes for which the funds can be used defined for the employees. Employees should also be required to get a receipt for any funds expended out of the petty cash fund.

6. Restrictive Endorsement   This control requires purchasing a restrictive endorsement stamp from the bank. As soon as checks are received, they should be restrictively endorsed.

7. Cash-Receipts Procedure   A formalized method for receiving cash should be instituted. Such a method has been described earlier in this chapter.

8. Bill-Paying Procedure   A formal procedure should be instituted for paying expenditures. Such a procedure has been described earlier in this chapter.

9. Independent Bank-Statement Reconciliation   The bank account should be reconciled by someone other than the individuals responsible for cash receipts, cash disbursements, and accounting for cash. In very small businesses this should be handled by the owner, and in larger businesses by the key financial officer. In addition to reconciling the bank statement, the reconciler should scrutinize the checks and deposits to ensure that:

- Deposits have been made on a timely basis.
- Deposits have been made intact.

- All checks have been made payable to someone and none made out to "cash."
- The payees appear to be reasonable.
- The amounts appear to be reasonable.

WHAT THREATS DO THE KEY CONTROLS ADDRESS?

The business threat represents a potential for loss. When determining which control to use and where to put it, the following two pieces of information need to be known about the threat:

1. *The point or points at which the threat is greatest.* For example, the threat of cash loss is greatest at the point where the cash is received. Normally this can be determined through some "negative" thinking, figuring out what can go wrong and where.
2. *The magnitude of the loss at each of these loss points.* This is an estimation based on the "what can go wrong" thinking.

The control or controls should then be placed at the point where the magnitude of loss is greatest. The money-management threat-reduction matrix (Figure 8-1) indicates what control is effective to reduce what threat. The placement of that control should be done in accordance with the above two-point procedure.

IF I CAN ONLY AFFORD TWO CONTROLS, WHAT SHOULD THEY BE?

Business cannot survive without cash planning. Although this may not be formal, it must be done or the business will either continually be in trouble or lose revenue for lack of appropriate use of idle cash. While essential, cash planning was not selected as one of the key controls because the business must first gain control of the movement of cash within the business.

The two key money-management controls are:

1. *Cash-receipts procedure.* The objective of this control is to ensure that there are standardized methods of receiving, recording, and

depositing cash. The fact that it is done the same way every day should make it readily apparent to the owner when unusual events occur. Even though the controls may not be as tight as they should be, a standardized procedure and an alert owner or manager can compensate for some of the cash-receipts vulnerabilities.

2. *Bill-paying procedure.* This provides the same level of control over cash disbursements as the cash-receipts procedure does over incoming cash. Again, smaller businesses cannot use controls in the same manner as do larger businesses but must rely on managerial oversight, which works best in a standardized environment. If events occur in the same manner all the time, it is much easier for the manager to supervise and oversee the functions.

HOW DO I KNOW THE CONTROLS WORK?

Almost all activities relate to the money-management activity. If this function can be well controlled, there is a control spillover to the other functions. Therefore it behooves management to spend extra time and effort on controlling this activity, especially when control over other activities appears weak.

Money management is closely tied to the financial records of the organization. This enables the company's management to use a series of financial evaluations in testing the correctness of the cash balances in addition to assessing the adequacy of the money-management controls.

Substantive Tests

The tests management can use to substantiate the correctness of the cash accounts are:

1. *Gross profit test.* This shows the comparison of inventory movement to cash receipts. Differences may mean either cash or inventory or both are missing.

2. *Financial statement ratios.* The percentage of expenditures used for each item in the financial statements should be compared against

previous periods and trends. For example, the amount spent for office supplies or repair should be shown as a percentage of expenditures. This can then be compared against previous months to help identify significant variations. Significant variations should be investigated.

3. *Control of financial accounts.* Areas of special concern to management should be identified. If money is involved, special accounts should be established so that these highly vulnerable uses of funds can be controlled. Examples of accounts of this type include:

   • Purchase returns
   • Damaged inventory
   • Petty cash expenditures
   • Stamps

4. *Surprise cash count or bank-statement reconciliation.* If management suspects problems, it should periodically do a surprise cash count of the petty cash fund or of other funds such as a cash drawer. In many instances when theft is involved, these accounts are out of balance for periods of time. This problem may be uncovered if the cash is counted without notice or if the bank statement is reconciled in the middle of the month by obtaining a special cutoff statement. Also, the fact that these two tests are done is itself a deterrent.

5. *Shoppers or spotters.* If the business suspects that all funds are not being properly recorded it should engage the services of a professional firm trained in spotting cash or merchandise thefts.

Internal Control Self-Assessment Checklist

The following self-assessment questionnaire (Checklist 5) is provided to assess the adequacy of money-management controls. This checklist covers both cash planning and cash receipts and disbursements. The receipts and disbursements controls have an immediate impact over the control of cash, while cash planning has a longer-term effect on the business. *Yes* answers are indicative of good control practices, and *no* answers represent potential vulnerabilities. If vulnerabilities are indicated, they should be investigated.

Checklist 5

CASH SELF-ASSESSMENT

Item	Yes	No	N/A	Comments
1. Is a comparison made between the initial record of cash receipts, on the one hand, and bank deposits and accounting entries on the other? Are unusual delays in depositing receipts investigated?				
2. Are there independent bank-statement reconciliations by someone other than the individuals responsible for cash disbursements and check signing?				
3. Do you require capital expenditure requests over a specified amount to be justified through cost-benefit analysis?				
4. Are all loans and major acquisitions approved by the chief executive officer?				
5. Are cash receipts deposited daily?				
6. Is excessive cash moved promptly to interest-bearing accounts?				
7. Has a business investment strategy been developed?				

9

controlling payroll and personnel activities

Since any system of internal control must be operated by people, it is logical that the success of the system will be determined by the quality and attitudes of the people who make up the system. Therefore, to set a foundation for exercising internal control, the business owner should attempt to staff the business with people who can be depended on to carry out the directions and goals of the business.

This chapter explores the impact of people on control and the ways people make control work. It identifies the threats to effective control because of people, as well as the controls that can be used through people to make control work. It is important that management establish a strong control environment. This chapter offers suggestions to management on strengthening the control environment in its business. In addition, some tests are provided to determine if people controls are working and to assess the effectiveness of the controls over the payroll and personnel activities.

WHAT IS THE MANAGEMENT PAYROLL AND PERSONNEL ACTIVITIES CHALLENGE?

Large losses in many businesses are attributable to mismanagement and abuse. These are situations in which managers and employees do not use their heads in decision making. For example, one food wholesaler was delivering groceries over such an extended area that the company spent more to deliver the goods than it received in sales-generated profits. In another business the employees sold a product at what they knew to be the wrong price, because it had that price marked on it. The employees never questioned changing the price. Case after case illustrates that, with the wrong employee attitude and inadequate control environment, losses occur.

Management's two major challenges in the payroll and personnel activities are first to create a strong control environment and second an environment in which employee work effectiveness is encouraged. The actions that management can take to make these happen include:

1. Strong Control Environment Perhaps the strongest control that management can initiate is the creation of a strong control environment. Employees follow both the words and actions of management. The clues they get from watching management are frequently more important than the messages they hear spoken by management. For example, if management says its wants strong controls but personally circumvents and fails to enforce them, the message transmitted to employees is that management really doesn't care about control.

A strong control environment is one that encourages and rewards employees for executing control. Without a strong control environment, application and event controls may be ineffective. After all, if managers override controls for their personal pleasure, then others may also. Controls, unless uniformly applied, are not effective.

Management creates a strong control environment by:

- Providing employees a memo or handbook on the business ethics the company expects the employees to follow.
- Personally following the business's control policies and procedures.
- Enforcing the control policies and procedures, which means reprimanding or discharging violators of the control policies.
- Not permitting the circumvention of normal controls, even when it becomes expedient to do so.
- Rewarding employees on their ability to follow and enforce controls.

We have all driven through areas where the local police enforce the speed limit. In these areas, we notice that automobiles slow down and closely follow the posted limit. In other towns, the speed limits are blatantly ignored. The town in which the people follow the speed limits has a strong control environment, while in the town in which the police and/or courts fail to enforce the rules they quickly become ignored by everyone.

2. Improved Work-Effectiveness Program   Work effectiveness is a concept fostered by industrial psychologists. It means an environment in which employees work at close to full capacity. In such an environment many of the traditional work constraints are removed.

A good work environment is important to control if people are to apply the controls realistically. In many organizations people apply the rule precisely instead of following the intent of the control. For example, a customer wanting to exchange an item, indicates that he or she is in a hurry to the sales clerk. The sales clerk states that the policy requires filling out certain forms, getting managerial approval, and so on. A clerk who felt confident in his or her work position might be willing to exchange the goods and then complete the paperwork afterwards. A clerk not feeling comfortable in the work position would follow the rules precisely. In the latter instance the rules are used as a crutch to protect one's position as opposed to doing what is in the best interest of the organization.

A work-effectiveness environment occurs in an organization where:

- Employees' advice and recommendations for improving their own jobs are solicited and implemented where possible.
- Employees are given authority to perform their work in any manner in which company policies and procedures are not violated.
- Employees are rewarded for their productivity and creativity, rather than for just being at work and following the rules.
- Jobs are structured to be large in scope.
- Employees are given realistic standards against which to measure their performance. This permits employees to know personally whether or not they are succeeding in fulfilling their job responsibilities.

In a good work environment, employees are free to work in the best interests of the organization. If controls are in the best interest, employees will follow and enforce them; if not in the best interest, then employees will either get exceptions from management or feel encouraged to recommend changing the controls. In this type of environment, controls tend to be more in line with the needs of the business because employees will not let the controls get out of synchronization with good business practices.

3. Hire Good Employees   The caliber and loyalty of employees is an essential element in a good control system. Organizations are better off to hire fewer people and pay them more money than to hire unproven workers. Time and effort expended in ensuring that the people hired are competent and effective is time well invested.

The practices that have proved effective in hiring good people include the following:

- Conduct a background check before hiring any employee. This involves checking on references and past employers.
- Establish reasonable performance standards. Employees should know what is expected of them and how their performance will be measured.
- Pay a fair day's wage for a fair day's work.
- Specify the skills needed to be effective in each job, and don't compromise on requiring those skills when hiring an employee.
- Train people to perform their jobs correctly.
- Evaluate employee performance regularly, and take those steps necessary to provide employees with needed skills to improve their performance.
- Offer employees jobs that are meaningful for their interests and desires.

WHY SHOULD I BE CONCERNED?
(THE THREATS)

The only real threat a business has is people. A computer — or any other piece of office equipment, for that matter — has yet to be taken to court and charged with stealing. Machines break, but rarely do they cause the business large losses. People are both the cause of control problems and the solution to control.

The specific people threats associated with payroll and personnel activities are:

1. Incorrect Salary Payments   One manager said that the most important task the business had to do was create the weekly payroll. If the business should fail to meet the payroll, the employees would leave and there would be no business. While the comment is somewhat face-tious, it is unfortunately true.

Incorrect salary payments to employees can result in a loss two ways. First, overpayments may not be recouped and thus become a loss. Second, improper payments can result in employee dissatisfaction, and perhaps termination with the company. Incorrect salary can occur because of:

• Incorrect reporting of hours worked
• Errors in calculation
• Incorrect calculation of deductions

2. Statutory Sanctions   Any owner of a small business is well aware of the myriad of forms required to be filed on employees. These include returns for unemployment taxes, FICA taxes, and federal withholding taxes; tax withholding forms; number-of-exemption forms; and probably another half dozen or more. Failure to file these forms or to fill them out properly can result in a penalty against the business. In some instances, large daily penalties can be assessed until the form is completed properly.

One business person stated that "I'm only in business to fill out federal, state, and local forms." While the prompt and correct filing of these forms does not improve the business's profitability, the failure to do so can decrease it. There appears little likelihood that the number and frequency of filing will be reduced.

3. Ineffective Use of Employees   Employees are one of the major resources of the organization. If they are used effectively, the organization should flourish and be profitable. If the organization fails to capitalize on the use of the individuals, profitability will be diminished.

The primary reasons employees fail to reach their potential include:

• Absence of direction
• Inadequate supervision
• Inadequate performance evaluation
• Inadequate performance measurement standards

- Inadequate training
- Inadequate delegation of authority

Most of the problems causing ineffective use of employees are correctable by management. The use of employees must be planned in the same manner as is cash and inventory. Good employee planning means that work is adequately planned, staff is of a sufficient size to perform the work reasonably, and the skill levels are matched to the tasks.

CONTROL RULE OF THUMB 23

If employee productivity is a problem, the cause of the problem is management.

---

4. Fraud and Theft Generally, people commit fraud and theft when management makes it easy for them to perform those acts. The stronger the controls, the less threat that occurs.

5. Loss of Customers or Trade Secrets It is not uncommon for an employee to leave one organization and go to another. While the loss of a good employee may be unfortunate, it is doubly so to lose customers, trade secrets, or both with that employee. In small businesses this is a very frequent occurrence. For example, in a service business an employee builds up a steady group of customers. The employee then forms his or her own business or goes with another similar business, taking all of those customers along. Thus, not only does the business lose a good employee, but it loses a reasonable portion of its business at the same time.

6. Employee Errors and Omissions Employee errors and omissions account for a major portion of business losses. Examples of such problems include:

- Miscalculation of invoices
- Offending customers
- Failure to properly record transactions
- Loss of transactions

Most errors and omissions are attributable to employee indifference, improper training, or inadequate supervision.

7. Loss of Skilled Employees Businesses can spend large amounts of money training employees. In some businesses it is weeks or even months before an employee becomes fully productive. Occasionally the business earns very little on that employee until he or she becomes productive. Thus the business may have invested hundreds or even thousands of dollars in training an employee before the business benefits from hiring that person.

If that employee leaves, the training and experience taught that employee leave also. A typical dilemma faced by a business is whether to pay an employee a few more dollars a month or lose the person. Economically it is almost always cheaper to pay a little more money and keep the employee. It is normally cheaper to pay equal to or greater than the prevailing wage in the industry for a needed skill than to lose that skill and have to hire a new employee.

HOW SHOULD I STRUCTURE MY STAFF?

The most important control consideration in assigning staff responsibilities is to prohibit anyone from being able to perform and conceal the same event; that is, after conducting an event, he or she then has an opportunity to adjust the accounting records of the business so that the event will not be disclosed. If this general rule of thumb is enforced, there is normally good segregation of duties.

In some small businesses this concept is difficult to implement, and it is recognized that an employee has the opportunity to conduct and conceal the same event. To minimize this from happening, management should install controls that compensate for the lack of the first control. Normally this is done by management oversight or by conducting those tests necessary to detect losses of this type.

WHAT ARE THE KEY CONTROLS?

There are two basic theories of control. One states that it is important to control transactions; the other that it is important to control people.

While there is probably merit in both arguments, control over people in small businesses is generally agreed to be more critical than control over transactions.

The types of controls that have proved effective in acquiring good people, keeping good people, and ensuring that they perform productive and honest work include:

1. Reference Checks It is advisable before hiring a new employee to check his or her background. Former employers and references should be contacted. Blocks of unexplained time on the employee's application may indicate a hidden dismissal or other problems. While employers must operate within constraints on probing a potential employee's background, it is important that the skill and integrity of a prospective employee be matched against those required for the open position.

2. Training Dr. W. Edward Deming, the chief architect of the Japanese industrial recovery after the Second World War, states that training is one of the attributes necessary for high-quality work. According to Dr. Deming, an employer should thoroughly train an employee and then ensure that the employee has mastered the necessary skills. Once it can be demonstrated that the employee fully comprehends the expected tasks, the employer should permit that employee to work with minimum supervision. If the employee is unable to complete the appropriate tasks after being adequately trained, then another employee should be acquired for that position.

3. Signed Time Cards The hours for which an employee is paid should be attested to by that employee. While it is reasonable to expect an employer to monitor the hours worked and paid, it is also important for the employee to sign a time card indicating the hours worked. Few individuals are willing to sign an untrue document.

4. Required Filing Calendar A filing calendar lists the dates on which federal, state, and local tax forms and tax deposits must be filed. Having this calendar in a prominent position and referring to it regularly should avoid the sanctions and penalties associated with missing required filings and deposits.

5. Employee Benefits   Some employee benefits are mandatory, and others are optional. For example, paying FICA taxes is a mandatory benefit, while vacation is an optional benefit. The objective of benefits is to encourage employee loyalty and stable employment. However, today many benefits are expected more than appreciated.

It is generally good for a business to provide benefits equal to or better than the benefits provided by other similar businesses. While these benefits cannot be expected to hold employees, they may encourage loyalty and discourage termination.

6. Fidelity Bonds   To protect businesses from losses, fidelity bonds should be carried on employees who handle money. Fidelity bonds cover larceny, theft, embezzlement, forgery, misappropriation, wrongful abstraction, and willful misapplication by employees acting alone or in collusion with each other. Although such bonds provide an inexpensive means of financial protection as well as a psychological deterrent to theft, only some 15 to 20 percent of all United States businesses use them. If fidelity bonds are used, employees should be reminded that bonding is an indication of the level of responsibility their position carries and thus an honor.

7. Position Procedures   Employees should know what is expected from them. Many businesses use position or job descriptions as a basis of defining the responsibilities and duties in specific job positions. While this may be uneconomical in small businesses, the employee should still be instructed on his or her role and responsibilities. It is normally advantageous for the owner to have at least formalized notes as to what is expected from an employee. These job descriptions should form the basis of employee performance reviews and thus the basis for merit increases.

8. Supervision   The role of supervisor should be well established. At a minimum it should include employee training, day-to-day direction, counseling, and evaluating employee performance. Good supervision normally leads to good control. Employees with too little direction tend to be the ones that abuse and defraud their employers.

9. Work-Effectiveness Programs   Employees are normally motivated by rewarding work. Work-effectiveness programs are designed to structure jobs so that employees are encouraged to work. While many small businesses cannot afford industrial psychologists and consultants to restructure their jobs, they can do the following to help improve job satisfaction:

- Give an employee responsibility over an entire job function
- Let the employee help structure the job
- Use exit interviews with employees to probe reasons for lack of job satisfaction

10. Payroll and Personnel Procedures Employees need to be treated fairly and equally. This is best accomplished by well-defined procedures that are equally applied. These include the methods of treating employees, paying employees, and offering them opportunities for advancement. Favoritism generally breeds discontent. Well-established and -enforced procedures encourage fairness in treating employees and consistency in the preparation, distribution, and accounting for employee wages and benefits.

WHAT THREATS DO THE KEY CONTROLS ADDRESS?

One expert on small business states that "when a small business fails, it's almost never due to outside circumstances but, rather, because management didn't do the right things." Invariably, the right thing means the establishment and execution of adequate people controls. Figure 9-1 illustrates the controls effective in reducing the major people threats. This matrix is designed to help the manager with control responsibilities select the more effective controls to reduce the threat of losses associated with employee activities.

IF I CAN ONLY AFFORD TWO CONTROLS, WHAT SHOULD THEY BE?

The one area that warrants meaningful controls is the payroll and personnel area. The types of controls that are most effective are those that build good employee relationships. Generally, satisfied, well-motivated

Key Controls \ Threats	Incorrect Salary Payments	Statutory Sanctions	Ineffective Use of Employees	Fraud/ Theft	Loss of Customers/ Trade Secrets	Employee Errors and Omissions	Loss of Skilled Employees
Reference checks				✔	✔	✔	
Training						✔	✔
Signed time cards	✔						
Required filing calendar		✔					
Employee benefits				✔	✔		✔
Fidelity bonds				✔			
Position procedures			✔			✔	
Supervision			✔	✔	✔	✔	✔
Work-effectiveness programs			✔		✔	✔	✔
Payroll and personnel procedures	✔	✔					

Figure 9-1 PAYROLL AND PERSONNEL THREAT-REDUCTION MATRIX

employees abide by and enforce controls. Dissatisfied employees are more likely to abuse and defraud the organization.

The two controls that should be considered first in this area are:

1. *Training.* If employees know what they are supposed to do and are given the appropriate tools, they are more likely to be satisfied and motivated employees. This assumes that training is appropriately structured and directed toward the work environment as opposed to generalized training. The more effective training is directed at providing the employees the skills they need to be effective on the job.

2. *Payroll and personnel procedures.* Developing detailed procedures on how to pay and interact with employees diminishes many personnel problems. Employees want to feel that they are being treated fairly. In addition, good policies prescribe the method in which pay is accumulated, recorded, and distributed. Such policies minimize cheating on payroll and the errors and omissions associated with the lack of controls.

HOW DO I KNOW THE CONTROLS WORK?

Employee work effectiveness, dedication, and honesty are important to the success of a business. Senior management should continually evaluate employee morale and satisfaction. Unhappy employees are troublesome employees for organizations. Experience has also shown that one of the major indicators of employee unhappiness is high turnover. If employee turnover exceeds 25 percent per year, the business turmoil will take a toll on both profitability and customer loyalty.

Senior management can perform two types of assessments on employee control. The first deals with the adequacy of the financial records associated with employees and their morale and satisfaction. These are substantive tests. The second type deals with the adequacy of the controls over payroll and personnel activities.

Substantive Tests

The tests that management can perform to evaluate the payroll and personnel activities are:

1. *Performance appraisals.* The performance appraisal should be a two-way assessment. It is recommended that management formally meet with employees at least once per year to discuss how things are going. Management should not only advise employees of their performance assessment and give them recommendations for improvement; it should also solicit their opinions on and recommendations for improving work conditions and morale.
2. *Exit interviews.* If an employee leaves an organization, it may be an unfortunate circumstance in that valuable skills, customers, trade secrets, or all three may be lost. Employers should attempt to sal-

vage as much as possible from a lost employee. One thing they may be able to retrieve is a frank and open assessment of the reasons the employee is leaving, the problems that might cause other employees to leave, and improvements that could be made to retain other needed employees.

3. *Gross payroll checks.* The amount of wages and benefits paid to employees should be easily verified. The employer should be able to total the stated salary of employees, plus any overtime or bonuses, to approximate the amount paid through the salary account. Employee benefits should be a portion of that and also easily verified. This verification may not be to the penny, but it should approximate and substantiate the salary and benefit payments.

4. *Smell test.* Management should be able to identify when employees are happy or unhappy. Body language, off-the-cuff remarks, and occasionally pointed remarks can indicate morale and personnel problems. People continually complaining about salary, work conditions, and hours are also indicators of employee dissatisfaction. When these conditions occur, management should look for means to improve morale, because that can normally be translated into improved productivity and thus improved profitability.

5. *Chamber-of-commerce coffee test.* Major corporations compare their salaries and benefits to equivalent positions in other like corporations. Smaller businesses can do that with local colleagues and friends. Generally these are people who would belong to a local chamber of commerce. The owner should attempt to get another business, to interchange salary and benefits information this will enable both businesses to ensure that the wages they are paying are equal to those from other employers in the community.

Internal Control Self-Assessment Checklist

Controls for many activities are *hard* controls: forms to complete, approvals to obtain, and comparisons to make. Employee controls, on the other hand, are often *soft* controls. These deal with relationships, benefits, and personal interactions. While employee controls may be more difficult to administer, they may also be more important.

Checklist 6 is designed to allow the manager to evaluate the adequacy of payroll and personnel controls. *Yes* answers to the checklist questions are indicative of good control practices, while *no* answers are representative of potential control vulnerabilities. *No* answers or qualified *yes* answers should be investigated to determine if the controls should be strengthened or if new controls should be added.

Checklist 6 PAYROLL AND PERSONNEL SELF-ASSESSMENT

Item	Response			
	Yes	No	N/A	Comments
1. Have procedures been established for hiring and terminating employees?				
2. Have policies been established for vacation pay, overtime pay, sick pay, and other similar benefits?				
3. Have policies been established regarding employee benefits and perquisites, such as the personal use of company cars?				
4. Have employees been assigned specific responsibilities regarding compliance with company policies and guidelines?				
5. Has responsibility been assigned to maintain personnel files including performance evaluations? (In the event of terminations, performance evaluation should be documented.)				
6. Are employees required to prepare and sign a time card?				
7. Has responsibility been assigned for preparing payroll and other employee-related tax returns?				
8. Have guidelines been established for determining payroll-account distributions to ensure that payroll gets charged to the appropriate account?				
9. Is there segregation of duties between personnel, timekeeping, and payroll preparation and distribution?				

Checklist 6   PAYROLL AND PERSONNEL SELF-ASSESSMENT
(Continued)

Item	Response			
	Yes	No	N/A	Comments
10. Are the payroll checks signed by someone other than the individual preparing the checks?				
11. Is a background check made on employees before they are hired?				
12. Are employee purchases properly controlled?				
13. Is the payroll-and-benefits system in compliance with governmental regulations?				
14. Are absences properly recorded?				

10

controlling profitability

The ultimate objective of any business is to make a profit. The controls discussed thus far in the book have addressed individual business activities. But many businesses overlook the necessity of integrating many aspects of the business into a cohesive, close working unit. This chapter discusses the management strategies that if not properly controlled can affect profitability. The controls that are effective in reducing threats to profitability are discussed and then related to the specific threats. The chapter provides some tests and assessments that management can do to verify whether its profitability is reasonable for the business.

WHAT IS THE MANAGEMENT PROFITABILITY CHALLENGE?

There is more to running a business than acquiring and selling a product. Obviously, having the right product and the right location are essential elements to success. On the other hand, it is not the lack of a good product that causes most businesses to fail. It is problems with the support activities and the lack of appropriate planning and financing that cause the early demise of nine out of ten business ventures.

Larger businesses tend to be successful because they employ a cadre of experts in multiple disciplines. When planning advice is needed, it's there. When accounting analyses are needed, accountants are available. Many smaller businesses do not have these luxuries.

In smaller businesses one or two key members of management must serve multiple roles. Unfortunately, some of these individuals have neither the skill nor the desire to perform many of the needed tasks. As a result, some of the important control strategies, such as budgeting, planning, and pricing, may not receive the appropriate attention. The net effect can be a loss of profit, or even, as previously discussed, the failure of the business.

The challenges faced by the small business in maintaining profitability without a full cadre of experts include:

- *Estimating profitability.* The successful business must have sufficient data to estimate the expected results of operation. Without this type of information, pricing becomes a guessing game. In addition, management cannot adequately plan on expansions, cash dividends, or working capital. The lack of good financial projections can severely handicap management's ability to build a successful operation. Many businesses have gone bankrupt because the owners made commitments without adequate financial information and that expansion cost them the business.

- *Acquiring the needed managerial skills.* The survival and growth of a business normally depend on the strategies adopted by management. For example, decisions to modernize, expand, relocate, add product lines, and drop product lines are all part of strategic and tactical planning. To perform these functions properly requires a wide range of skills. Management's challenge is to hire, buy, borrow, or beg the necessary skills to ensure that it is adequately prepared for today's and tomorrow's competitive environment.

- *Acquiring adequate decision-making information.* Good decisions require good information. For example, if management wants to minimize inventory, it needs current and accurate information on inventory status. If management wants to buy only those products that are selling, it needs timely and accurate sales information. If management wants to follow up on receivables, it needs timely and accurate information on collections. Many businesses survive on managerial intuition. However, sooner or later intuition will fail. The question will be: Can the business survive the losses associated with poor management intuition?

These are some of the most difficult challenges facing the small business. The staff in the larger business takes the time to work through the alternate strategies in order to pick the one with the highest probability of success. The staff is then available to support the implementation of those strategies. Smaller businesses must use alternate methods to provide them with the highest probability of success.

WHY SHOULD I BE CONCERNED?
(THE THREATS)

The concerns that management should have about profitability are often missing in a small business. The problem with controls over profitability is that the threat must be recognized first before the control can be installed to reduce it. If the threat is not recognized, then management will see no need to install the control.

The specific profitability threats of concern to a business include:

1. Products Incorrectly Priced   Many businesses sell their products for less than what they bought them for. Others sell at a price higher than what they paid for the product but still lower than the total costs of selling the product. This happens because a business may not know or perform the calculations necessary to determine a reasonable selling price. Other businesses forget about selling and administrative expenses and worry only about a markup on costs. Unfortunately, businesses cannot stay in existence for very long when they begin to sell products below cost. The more typical case is the business that sells some products at a loss and others at a profit.

The selling price for a product should be calculated as follows:

Cost of product	$1.00
Selling expenses (includes sales commission, delivery, and so on)	.60
Plus administrative and overhead costs	.40
Total cost to the business to sell the product	$2.00
Add 20 percent desired profit	.40
Selling price of product	$2.40

Using this formula, the business predetermines the profit it wants and then includes that in the selling price. This is a practical way for a small business to ensure that it will achieve a reasonable profit. While other pricing methods can be used, this simple approach will control the profitability of the business.

2. Inadequate Cash   Businesses need cash flow to survive. They also need cash for modernization, expansion, marketing campaigns, and so forth. If a business stands still too long, it may be surpassed by its competitors.

Few businesses are fortunate enough to have excess cash available for use when needed. If the business is profitable the distribution of the profits to the owners can reduce the working capital and thus excess cash. If cash is not available through the generation of profits, then the business needs to borrow funds or sell stock if there is a market for the stock. The accumulation of cash normally involves planning.

3. Inappropriate Management Decisions A decision made by an individual member of business management will be based on his or her:

• Skills
• Work experience
• Access to the appropriate internal information
• Access to the appropriate external information
• Willingness to commit the organization in a new direction or reduce an existing strategy

The individual who lacks any or all of these, may make decisions inappropriate for the betterment of the business.

4. Failure to Benefit from Automation Many businesses are pricing themselves out of the market due to their ineffective means of doing business. For example, computers can be acquired to automate office systems, which may significantly reduce the cost of those systems. Depending on the business, other means of automation can be used to cut costs and increase quality. The failure of the business to take advantage of new technology may first result in loss of profits and second in loss of the business.

The reluctance to move to automation is twofold: first, the equipment may be expensive; and second and perhaps more important, new skills need to be acquired. Many owners or managers of small businesses do not want to commit the time and effort to learning a new skill. In the back of their mind, they cling to the belief that they can be just as efficient using manual methods. Unfortunately, many of the basic industries in the world have had to learn costly lessons from the Japanese in the use of new methods and modern technology.

It is much easier for a business to automate its processes when it is profitable and has the time. If the automation of competitors reduces profits, businesses are reluctant to expend those scarce profits for automation. Many businesses are now operating in a survival mode but are unaware of it because of the lack of adequate external business information.

5. Company Improperly Organized Work flow and decision making are partially dependent on organizational structure. In very small businesses the owner or manager may be involved in too many decisions, and this can inhibit employee work effectiveness. In larger organizations too little time and effort may have been spent on developing a good organizational structure. Again, operational efficiency may be affected by this lack of organizational planning.

A good organizational structure is one of the strongest controls available to small and medium-sized business organizations. Organizational controls are both financial and operational. Financial controls relate to the safeguarding of the organization's assets, while operational controls relate to the effectiveness, economy, and efficiency in methods of operation.

The lack of organizational controls can result in:

- One individual being able to both perform and conceal the same event
- Decision-making bottlenecks (such as no one being able to make a decision until the boss returns)
- Ineffective or inefficient work flow (for example, work must flow through three or four departments before action is taken)
- Responsibility voids (such as no one having responsibility for the acceptance of returned goods or for returning goods to a vendor)
- Inadequate supervision (for example, one worker reports to two, three, or even four different people for day-to-day direction)

HOW SHOULD I ORGANIZE MY STAFF?

Organizational structure is one of the most important controls for a small business. It is important for both financial and operational controls. Therefore, when determining how to organize the business, management needs to consider the control implications of the organizational structure.

Chapters 4 through 9 have provided guidance on how to organize along functional lines (for example, inventory, cash receipts, and so on). These guidelines were primarily directed at financial controls. Those chapters provided a series of tests that the owner could undertake to substantiate the financial balances. These tests can be used to compensate for the lack of extensive organizational division of responsibility controls. It is recognized that the size or caliber of staff may not make some of the desirable division-of-responsibility controls practical.

Organizing for operational effectiveness is equally as important as organizing for financial control. The success of the business may be dependent on its responsiveness to customer needs. Organizational structure has a direct effect on responsiveness.

While it is difficult to develop a single organizational structure that has universal applicability, some general guidelines may prove helpful:

- *Operational Guideline 1 — Center an entire work function around a single individual.* It has been said that today's society is an IWIN society. This stands for *I Want It Now.* People are reluctant to deal with businesses that pass customer requests or needs from person to person within the organization. Customers and clients want the first individual they talk with to provide them the service, product, or need that they desire.

    This organizational principle states that within reasonable limits a single individual should have the necessary authority to act. For example, if a customer returns a product to the sales person from whom he or she purchased the product, that sales person should be able to make all of the routine returns and adjustments. It is normally far cheaper to the business to lose some funds because of a poor decision at this level than to lose customers because a decision could not be made.

- *Operational Guideline 2 — Use supervisors to train and evaluate.* If the Guideline 1 is followed, employees will be delegated the necessary authority to act. Thus it will not be necessary for supervisors to perform part of the employees' work. In other words, an employee will not have to keep asking a supervisor for permission to perform routine acts, as is frequently the case in department stores, where customer checks must be okayed before being cashed or accepted.

When supervisors are freed from performing the work of each employee, they will have additional time to supervise. This time should be spent on training employees how to do their jobs right and on evaluating their work performance. This is the true role of a supervisor. If employees cannot do their work properly, then one might assume they have been inadequately trained or that the results of their work have not been evaluated by their supervisors.

- *Operational Guideline 3—Minimize middle management.* When the Guidelines 2 and 3 are followed, the need for middle management disappears. Many businesses have been accused of having too much management. This is normally attributable to the fact that employees are not permitted to perform their jobs. When management must do routine work, the need for management increases. Then it takes two people to do the job of one, because the organizational structure has not been properly developed.

If these three principles are followed, the company will derive some very positive benefits. First, there are fewer high-paid management jobs, which means more profit for the business. Second, employees have more control over their day-to-day work, which increases employee satisfaction, morale, and work effectiveness. Third, because employees are more productive and there are fewer managerial jobs, employees can be paid more. This means less turnover and happier employees, which tends to make for better customer relations.

WHAT ARE THE KEY CONTROLS?

The most important profitability control is the proper organization of the business. While this is a control, it also involves managerial decisions. Constant study and evaluation by senior management are required to ensure that the organizational structure is consistent with the current needs of the business.

Organizational structure should be changed as the business changes and as people change. It is good policy to build an organization around the strength of the people within that organization. People are much better suited to some functions than others, so management must make the organizational structure changes that capitalize on the strength of its employees.

The key controls that help improve profitability by being supportive of the organizational structure are:

1. Budgeting Budgeting is a by-product of planning, which estimates income and expenditures and then tracks actual income and expenditures against the budgeted amount. Budgets normally cover a one-year period, divided into monthly increments for comparison purposes. Budgets are valuable only when (1) they are a by-product of planning and (2) they are used as a control.

Budgeting can be as general or specific as management desires. For example, budgets could be prepared that estimate the total sales by month, sales by group of products, or sales by individual product. The more detailed the budget, the greater the control it provides, but the more time and effort needed to develop and track it.

Budgeting is an accounting control. If management is uncomfortable with accounting, the company can engage the services of its independent accountant to help develop and track a budget. Normally the time and effort expended on budgeting will be paid back manyfold through the company's increased ability to adjust to changing business conditions. Budgeting is also an extremely helpful control for avoiding cash-flow problems.

2. Cost Accounting Cost accounting is the part of accounting that develops the detailed costs associated with a product. The objective of cost accounting is to provide management with information on the costs associated with buying or selling a product. The process involves accumulating and allocating all cost data connected with manufacturing, purchasing, or selling.

Management needs good cost information in order to properly price a product. If the costs are not properly identified, management may be selling products for less than the costs associated with selling that product. On the other hand, management may be overpricing products, which puts the company at a competitive disadvantage in the marketplace. It is important for an organization in a competitive business to know what leeway it has in making price changes. It may be better to let a competitor sell a product below the company's cost than to attempt to match that price. Regardless, management must know whether the company is making or losing money on each sale.

CONTROL RULE OF THUMB 24

It is not true that volume sales on a product will make up for what you lose on an individual sale. The more you sell of a loss leader, the more you will lose.

---

3. Business Planning   One of the major reasons cited for business failure is the lack of planning. Businesses operating on a day-to-day basis are at a competitive disadvantage in their marketplace. Planning provides them with the survival strategies necessary to stay in business over an extended period of time.

Yet planning is the one activity that most businesses never have time for. The dilemma raised by many managers is that if they have to run at full speed just to keep up with the day-to-day pressures of business, how are they going to find time to plan? This logic leads to the early demise of many businesses.

Planning causes business management to address the following type of questions:

- What type of product should I be selling in the future?
- Are the needs of my customer base changing?
- Should I be providing additional services to my customers?
- Am I selling products or services that are no longer economical for me to offer or perform?
- Am I performing services in-house that would be cheaper if I were to contract them out?
- Is my business staff properly organized?
- What skills do my people need to be more effective?
- Is my advertising program effective?
- Is this an advantageous time for me to sell the business?
- Is this an advantageous time for me to acquire another business?
- Am I paying too much in taxes?

The answers to these and similar questions are needed to develop a business plan. Larger organizations develop both one-year and five-year plans. For smaller businesses a one-year plan is usually sufficient. Normally the planning should begin about three to six months before the end of the year. Management then adjusts the plan during the year as business conditions change. In conjunction with developing the plan, management should prepare a budget.

4. Systems Planning   Systems planning relates to the flow of information through the business and is concerned with both financial and operational controls. A systems plan identifies input transactions and then shows how they flow through the business to produce the desired results.

Systems planning requires selecting the tools necessary for processing the information. These include:

- Business computers
- Office equipment
- Office furniture, fixtures, and supplies
- Physical location of people, work stations, and departments
- Location and arrangement of inventory
- Forms, filing cabinets, and record-keeping methods

Larger businesses may have experts in systems development, who are frequently called *systems analysts*. In smaller businesses this type of work is normally performed by the owner or manager. Unfortunately, many owners are not properly qualified to perform that work.

Businesses can get help in systems planning from any or all of the following sources:

- Trade and business associations
- Computer hardware and software vendors
- Office supply businesses
- Business forms sales people
- Business equipment sales people
- Accountants and consultants

Many systems problems are not readily apparent to the owner or manager. Employees tend to assume that the boss expects them to perform the work in accordance with the systems structure. Thus, while many employees know that the system is bad, they live with it without complaint. It behooves management periodically to evaluate the systems flow in the business by having discussions with employees, making personal observations, or engaging a consultant.

5. Consultants Businesses should make extensive use of consultants. Larger organizations have the resources to hire staffs with expertise in all needed areas. Smaller businesses do not have this luxury. Therefore, they must compensate for the lack of necessary skills by engaging outside consultants.

A smart business should develop a group of consultants from these fields of expertise:

- Accounting
- Taxes
- Law
- Business systems
- Advertising
- Inventory and marketing
- Insurance and benefits
- Investments and cash management

One of the arguments raised for not engaging a large cadre of consultants is cost. On the other hand, many of these consultants are free or available for only minimal cost. For example, bankers and stockbrokers provide cash management and investment advice at no cost. Computer vendors and form manufacturers will give systems advice at no cost. Many insurance agents will offer insurance and benefit planning at no cost. Lawyers will normally work with the business for a moderate retainer fee, such as $50 a quarter, which covers all but the most extensive legal assistance. Accountants charge by the amount of work performed and once engaged will normally answer a variety of questions at no additional cost.

The small business building a cadre of consultants has a much better opportunity to survive in the marketplace and compete against larger businesses with their staffs of full-time experts. The small business does not have to pay the large cost of maintaining a consulting staff but can get that same caliber of services. Many times, getting the right advice at the right time provides a competitive edge.

CONTROL RULE OF THUMB 25
Decisions based on fact are right much more often than are decisions based on intuition.

WHAT THREATS DO THE KEY CONTROLS ADDRESS?

The major profitability threat is that management will overlook a good opportunity to make a profit. I have subdivided this general threat into specific threats that can be addressed. Figure 10-1 illustrates the controls a business can use to reduce the profitability threats. This matrix can be used in strategic planning to help develop strategies that will make the business more profitable.

IF I CAN ONLY AFFORD TWO CONTROLS, WHAT SHOULD THEY BE?

Directly controlling profitability is an area overlooked by many businesses. Many businesses rely on an increasing volume of sales as the means to increase profitability. In reality there are other means that can significantly affect the bottom-line.

Threats / Key Controls	Products Incorrectly Priced	Inadequate Cash	Inappropriate Management Decisions	Failure to Benefit from Automation	Company Improperly Organized
Budgeting	✔	✔	✔		
Cost accounting	✔				
Business planning	✔		✔		✔
Systems planning				✔	✔
Consultants	✔	✔	✔	✔	✔

Figure 10-1 PROFITABILITY THREAT-REDUCTION MATRIX

The two controls that prove most advantageous to the long-run survival and profitability of the business are:

1. *Cost accounting*. If a business doesn't know what its products cost it can never be sure of the amount of profit, if any, it will make. Knowing all the costs provides the basic input needed for business survival. Managers without good information will be as successful in planning profitability as a duck hunter is at shooting in the dark.

2. *Business planning*. Businesses need guidance and direction just as people do. While some businesses will be successful using owner judgment and intuition, many will not. Planning is a methodical approach to establishing and achieving business goals. The more competitive the industry, the greater the need for planning. It is difficult to compete successfully against well-planned businesses without also using planning as a strategy.

CONTROL RULE OF THUMB 26

If you don't have a plan to tell where you are going, you will probably not get there; and if you do, you won't know you've arrived.

HOW DO I KNOW THE CONTROLS WORK?

The two greatest tests for determining whether profitability controls work are failure and bankruptcy. However, you need to know how well you are doing before these two undesirable business conditions occur. As in any area, competition is a good judge of how well you are doing. For example, if you were a runner, you might feel very competent about your ability until the first race. Thinking you are a good runner but then coming in last in a race would be an eye-opening experience, providing feedback on your capabilities. Businesses need the same type of assessment to determine if they are living up to their profit potential. This assessment can be done through tests or by evaluating internal controls.

If the business is profitable, the controls are working. There is no magic formula for profitability, or any one control that will ensure profitability. Controls are merely the method used by management to run its business better. If the controls are performing properly and management is using them correctly, then the probability of growing profitability increases.

The tests that management can conduct to substantiate the functioning of the controls are limited. On the other hand, the control assessment may give a better appreciation of the functioning of the controls. Well-controlled businesses in general appear to be more profitable than those poorly controlled.

Substantive Tests

The tests that a business can conduct to determine if it is meeting its profit potential include:

1. Profitability Comparison within Industries Businesses within a specific industry tend to cluster around certain profit levels. For example, supermarkets typically generate 1 to 3 percent gross profit. It is recommended that you acquire this type of information, which is normally available from industry trade associations. Then, based on your location, characteristics, volume, and so forth, compare your business to other like businesses. If your profitability is above average, you can feel you are doing something right; if below average, remedial action may be necessary to boost profits.

2. Profitability Trends One of the best competitors to compare yourself to is yourself. Increasing sales or profits is indicative of a well-run business that's getting better. On the other hand, declining sales or profits is a sign for alarm and a call for immediate attention to the business. If declining sales, profits, or both cannot be remedied, you may have no business within the next few years.

3. Market Research It is periodically advisable to examine your customer base to determine how you are doing. This can be done by holding personal interviews if customers are in the store, or by conducting formal surveys sent to your customers in questionnaire form. Sometimes surveys are a routine part of doing business, such as providing hotel or motel guests the opportunity to comment about service. If customers are unhappy with the service, this most likely affects the business's profitability or may affect it shortly because the customer will stop being a customer.

4. Vendor Survey   Your vendors interact with many businesses in your industry. They can observe your buying practices, your competitors' buying practices, and other attributes of business. It is advisable periodically to sit down with your vendors and have them assess your business, business practices, buying practices, and so on. These "report cards" may provide you clues as to areas in which you could significantly increase your business practices and thus profitability.

5. Consultant Evaluation   Periodically it is helpful to invite a consultant to assess the way in which you conduct your business. Selecting the proper consultant is important. He or she should be someone who knows the industry in which you operate and perhaps even your specific business, although this is not necessary. Frequently an excellent consultant is your business's accountant. Many accountants work within one industry, and for this reason it may be advisable to engage an accountant who is knowledgeable within your industry.

6. Achievement of Planned Profits   Businesses should establish profitability goals. If those goals are achieved, management should feel reasonably content that it has installed the appropriate controls and that those controls are functioning. Failure to achieve the desired profitability should indicate to management that the controls probably aren't providing warning sufficient to make the adjustments necessary to achieve goals.

7. Critical-Success-Factor Ranking   A critical success factor is an important managerial objective. For example, achieving the profitability of X percent, operating with an employee turnover rate of less than Y percent, and acquiring a new product line can all be considered critical success factors. Management should be asked to define these critical success factors and then rank them in importance. The ranking should be consolidated to produce one set of critical success factors for the business. Next, management should determine the type of controls or control information that would be helpful in accomplishing these critical success factors. Lastly, it must be determined whether that control information is available. How well the existing controls match those needed to accomplish the critical success factors is an assessment of the completeness and effectiveness of the profitability controls.

Internal Control Self-Assessment Checklist

There are many controls that a business can use to help its profitability. Checklist 7 addresses many of these controls. While a specific control may not have a direct relation to profitability, those businesses that utilize the previously described profitability controls appear to be more profitable than those that don't. *Yes* answers are indicative of controls that help increase profitability, while *no* answers represent potential control activities that management should consider as a means for improving profitability.

CONTROL RULE OF THUMB 27
The final test in assessing the adequacy of any part of the business is the amount of profit generated.

Checklist 7   PROFITABILITY SELF-ASSESSMENT

		Response		
Item	Yes	No	N/A	Comments
1. Are procedures established for making appropriate financial statement accruals based on unmatched receiving reports, and, where appropriate, unmatched purchase orders?				
2. Are budgets prepared, reviewed, and adjusted when necessary?				
3. Has the method of depreciating fixed assets been determined based on desired profitability?				
4. Is a periodic review made of the reasonableness of the lives assigned to classes of property, of deferred costs, and of the depreciation and amortization methods?				
5. Is a cost accounting system used to determine the actual cost of products and services?				
6. Have estimated gross and net profit percentages been determined?				
7. Is the selling price of products and services based on the projected targets for gross and net profits?				
8. Have adequate physical controls been installed (for example, fences, restricted-access storerooms, guards, inspection of personnel, independent storeroom clerks)?				
9. Are physical controls consistent with the value of the items being protected?				
10. Are cash-flow analyses prepared regularly?				
11. Are loan and other legal agreements reviewed by legal counsel prior to signing?				

Checklist 7   PROFITABILITY SELF-ASSESSMENT (Continued)

Item	Yes	No	N/A	Comments
			Response	
12. Are key financial ratios and statistics prepared and reviewed regularly?				
13. Does the firm's accountant approve all accounting procedures and methods, such as depreciation?				
14. Is the business's independent public accountant asked to comment annually on the adequacy of business policies and procedures?				
15. Does the business retain a group of advisors, such as a banker, stockbroker, insurance agent, computer hardware/software firm, and so forth?				
16. Does the chief executive officer meet at least annually with these advisors to discuss the adequacy of business policies and procedures and to seek recommendations?				
17. Are the reasons for returned merchandise identified and summarized for management analysis?				
18. Is competitive bidding required on purchases (where applicable)?				
19. Are labor-intensive information-processing functions automated?				

11

controlling record keeping

Most of the information necessary to keep informed regarding business finances and progress of operations comes from the accounting records. To be of greatest value, this information must be reliable, complete, and readily available. Accounting information can be used to answer such diverse questions as "What was last year's advertising expenses?" or "How many of product X do we have in stock?"

If the accounting information provides accurate information about past and present operations, the owner or manager can:

1. Estimate as nearly as possible the amount of sales for a future period.
2. Estimate the possible expenses connected with those sales.
3. Determine if the company will need extra cash.
4. Determine, if a loan is necessary, how it can be repaid.
5. Make other needed analyses about income and expense.

This chapter discusses the threats and controls associated with an organization's record-keeping system. Information is the lifeblood of many businesses. Therefore, discussions include some of the record-keeping alternatives including the computer, that are available to businesses. The chapter also explains how a business person can evaluate the effectiveness of and controls over his or her record-keeping system.

WHAT IS THE MANAGEMENT RECORD-KEEPING CHALLENGE?

Studies of business failures show that frequently failure can be attributed to inadequate records. Specifically, lack of information can prevent a business person from properly evaluating the status of the business. The manager of the small business should therefore spend whatever effort and money are necessary to maintain an adequate record-keeping system. Of particular importance is the documentation of information for federal tax purposes.

Other important uses of adequate records are to request credit and to substantiate claims about the business. For these reasons the business may require the services of an independent auditor. The banks may require a certification or transmittal letter from a certified public accountant or chartered accountant regarding the adequacy of the financial statements. To properly perform an audit, records are necessary to prove transactions.

Records must also be relevant, verifiable, and accurate if they are to be used as a basis for decision making. Accurate records lessen the probability of making costly errors and missing profitable opportunities. With the data contained in the financial records, it is possible to construct liquidity and profitability ratios to reveal trends within the company and to compare them with norms published for other like businesses. Information on fixed costs and contribution margin per unit of sales can be used to calculate how many units must be sold to break even. Records of past expenditures provide the basis for formulating budgets for the future. Owners or managers no longer need to manage "by the seat of their pants" if they are willing to invest the effort necessary to implement an efficient record-keeping system.

Many of the tests recommended in earlier chapters need data produced by the record-keeping system. Some of the information is readily available from most record-keeping systems, while other data needed for the tests require the establishment of special reporting systems. The management of the business, together with the accountant, should determine the tests that are advantageous for control purposes and then should establish a record-keeping system to provide that data.

WHY SHOULD I BE CONCERNED? (THE THREATS)

By their nature, smaller businesses have an insufficient number of employees to permit extensive division of responsibilities. Most good control practices assume adequate segregation of functions. Such a structure may not exist in smaller organizations, especially those in which the manager exercises virtually all authority and control.

Frequently, the owner or manager does not realize that there are simple commonsense steps that can be undertaken to provide strict expense and cash controls, guard against defalcations (embezzlements), and highlight the existence of unsound business and managerial practices. Many of these result from having a record-keeping system that is economical and easy to implement and operate. Even with a limited staff, effective records can be maintained without requiring excessive effort.

A business enterprise should be interested in establishing control where it is economically feasible to protect such assets or to improve the operational efficiency of the business. Each business has unique areas of concern and must decide on these individually. Evaluating the threats in each business activity is the recommended method for determining those areas in which record-keeping controls will be most economical.

The record-keeping threats that need to be assessed in determining the type of system to build and the controls to install include:

1. System Too Costly A record-keeping system that is overly elaborate and involves a great deal of paperwork will not function well in most businesses. Many of the theoretical systems described in accounting and auditing texts do not work in the small to medium-sized business. When the employees of the business do not feel that the record-keeping system improves their work effectiveness, that system is probably too costly.

The costs associated with an ineffective and inefficient record-keeping system include:

- Time spent completing unnecessary or lengthy forms
- Extra people time recording unneeded information
- Customer dissatisfaction due to delays and potential loss of customer business
- Loss of employee time complaining about the system

2. Data Unreliable   Decisions are made and actions taken based on the information produced by the record-keeping system. For example, the record-keeping system will indicate when a particular item is almost out of stock or that a product is frequently reordered. If the record-keeping system indicates that the cost to sell a product is X dollars, then the selling price may be based on that cost information. When the information on which those decisions are based is inaccurate or incomplete, the decision may be wrong. The wrong item or quantity of inventory may be ordered or the wrong price established on a product.

3. Records Not Used as a Working Tool   Record-keeping systems should be designed to support the work flow of the business. For example, the recording of a sale for accounting purposes should be the same recording done for customer purposes. When several copies of the records are needed, they should be prepared using carbon copies or reproduced through recording equipment. As little effort as possible should be expended making entries into the system simply for record-keeping purposes. Generally, if the information is not needed for some business function, the data should not be recorded. The possible exception to this rule is the general ledger of the business, which is used for preparation of financial statements.

If not part of the regular work of the business, the record keeping may result in:

- Incomplete recording of data
- Late recording of data
- Inaccurate recording of data

4. Results Not Understood   One of the greatest threats to managing a small business is that managers will prepare reports and financial statements and then not understand the meaning of the information on those reports. This is common in many businesses. The owner or manager will receive and read the financial statement but won't really understand it. A few items will be meaningful, such as sales and net profit, and most of the individual line items will be clear, but the owner or manager won't know how to use that information for control purposes.

This condition usually occurs for either or both of the following reasons:

- Person using the financial statements is unskilled in the use of those statements.
- Person preparing the statements does not take the time and effort to explain the information and its meaning.

5. System Complex to Use   It is very common for the people preparing a system to be more highly skilled and motivated than the people using it. This results in a system design that is too sophisticated for the skill or motivation level of the people using that system. There is a direct relationship between the complexity of the system and the reliability of the data collected by that system.

Many business problems involving inaccurate recording of data are directly attributable to the complexity of the system. For example, the system may require individuals to perform multiplication, extensive addition, and other arithmetic operations. Sometimes the employee has to look up prices or perform other error prone tasks. The net result is that the data recorded are erroneous. Experience has shown that most errors favor the customer.

HOW SHOULD I STRUCTURE MY STAFF?

Employee behavior has a significant impact on the success of the business. In the establishment of a record-keeping system, the manager should consider employees' skills and attitudes and the importance that management places on internal control in record keeping. If the employees do not understand the system or its importance, problems will incur. In these instances, management will have to turn its attention toward record-keeping systems instead of toward the problems associated with making a profit for the business.

Management has three basic decisions to make regarding a record-keeping system. First, what type of record-keeping system does the business need, including the chart of accounts? Second, how much, if any, of the system will be automated? Third, what types and frequencies of reports will be produced by the record-keeping system and how those reports will be used?

The System

The record-keeping system need not be complex. One of the most useful guides to setting up and maintaining books for a small business can be obtained free of charge from the Internal Revenue Service. Although the procedures suggested by the IRS are designed primarily to ensure that adequate information is available for preparing accurate tax returns, these same procedures provide sufficient information for controlling operations.

Establishment of a double-entry system of record keeping provides built-in checks and balances that assure accuracy. First, transactions are entered in a journal. At a minimum, most businesses have a separate journal for recording sales, purchases, cash disbursements, and cash receipts. Summary totals from each of these journals are posted monthly to the general ledger, which contains all of the business's permanent and temporary accounts. Temporary accounts such as expenses and revenues are closed at the end of each accounting period. In contrast, asset, liability, and owner's equity accounts are maintained as permanent accounts.

Double-entry bookkeeping is self-balancing. Every transaction is shown as a debit entry in one account and a credit entry in another. When journal entries are posted to the general ledger, the total of debit entries will equal the total of credit entries if transactions have been recorded properly. Any inequality signals an inaccuracy in the records and indicates that corrective action should be taken, especially if the difference is material. Once the ledger is in balance, a balance sheet and income statement can be prepared easily.

Manual or Automated Method

Record-keeping systems can be automated in many ways. The systems are composed of three basic parts: input or data collection, then the processing of business information, and finally the output reports produced by the system.

In smaller businesses very effective manual systems are available. One of the more effective is the one-write system. A pegboard, or one-write system of accounting, offers small companies a potential cost saving in record keeping. With this system it is possible to post information on three records in one writing by aligning three records on pegs and using paper printed with spot carbon. A sales transaction, for example, could be fully documented this way. One copy of the record would be used for an accounts receivable journal, another for a sales journal, and the last for the customer statements. The same type of system could be used for cash disbursements.

Although this system uses journals and ledgers as do the more traditional systems, the journals consist of source documents rather than entries copied from source documents. In smaller businesses the advantages of the one-write system normally outweigh the shortcomings.

As businesses become larger, a variety of automated input recording devices can be used. Among the more widely used are electronic cash registers. Some of these can collect information in electronic media for entry into automated systems. Other electronic cash registers are connected directly to computers and can pass information to and receive it from the computer. This is frequently helpful in checking customer credit.

Businesses with over twenty-five employees can normally benefit from the use of a computer. The types of business systems that can be processed by computer include:

- Inventory control
- Replenishment of inventory
- Accounts receivable
- Accounts payable
- General ledger
- Payroll

Small business computers do not require extensive training to operate. They are not much more sophisticated than some of the electronic cash registers. The individual operating the computer should have approximately one week of schooling and then time to learn applications through on-the-job training.

The characteristics that provide good control in computer systems include:

- Easy-to-read user manuals
- *User-friendly systems* (systems that provide clues if things are wrong, give suggestions on how to make them right, and offer help on what to do next when the person gets in trouble)
- Adequate backup so that if a system problem occurs, not much time and effort is lost in reconstructing the processing
- Availability of a dealer or sales person to help the business should it get into trouble (which is particularly important during the first few weeks and months of operation)

Frequency of Reports

The objective of record-keeping systems is to produce information for both tax and decision-making purposes. The type of information needed for tax purposes is specified by the Internal Revenue Service and can be defined by an organization's independent accountant.

Among the financial statements that a business should produce for business purposes include:

- Balance sheet
- Statement of income and expense (showing month-to-month or year-to-year comparison for each item in the statement)
- Cash-flow statement (showing source and use of cash)
- Payroll report (showing employee earnings and deductions for tax purposes)
- Inventory status (showing balances and uses)
- Accounts receivable aging report (showing customers, account balance, and amount of time elapsed since the item was charged)

- Marketing information (analytical information showing sales by product, customer, area, and so on)

The use of reports, forms, and records by the business should be kept at a minimum. All items should serve a useful purpose relating to company objectives, be simple to understand, and be designed in light of all possible uses. The manager must decide what information is needed to operate the business efficiently and implement a record-keeping system that produces only that type of information.

WHAT ARE THE KEY CONTROLS?

The objective of the controls is to make sure a record-keeping system is developed that:

- Is simple and direct without sacrificing any essential records
- Produces current information in a form that is easy to understand
- Is tailored to meet the specific requirements of the business
- Is economical to implement and operate
- Is a working tool for the employees of the business

The specific controls that help achieve these record-keeping objectives are:

1. Customized Systems and Forms   It is generally uneconomical for businesses to develop information systems from scratch. The same is true for forms, reports, and input-gathering processes. It is far more economical to purchase or acquire a generalized system and then adapt it to specific purposes, thus customizing the system to the organization. Customization involves:

- Using company name or logo on forms
- Preparing instructions or procedures for the organization using the system
- Optimizing the system for the skills of the people using it
- Eliminating unneeded features
- Training employees in the proper use of the system

2. Double-Entry Bookkeeping Double-entry bookkeeping is the standard method for recording financial information. Public accountants use the results of double-entry bookkeeping to prepare financial statements. The extra effort required to perform this kind of bookkeeping is normally offset by the additional control gained by the firm's accountant. Business managers unfamiliar with double-entry bookkeeping should either read a basic accounting textbook or take a course in elementary accounting to familiarize themselves with its principles and concepts.

3. Multiple Use of Records Good record-keeping systems require recording transactions only once. Reposting transactions two or more times is normally a waste of people time. The system itself should be established so that multiple use can be made of a single recording. Automated equipment facilitates this process in larger organizations. The advantages to recording only once are that more effective use can be made of people time and that the probability of errors due to reposting the same information twice or more decreases.

4. Prenumbered Forms Record-keeping systems are designed to control the information they process. Much of that information will be processed either as input or output. Both can be controlled through the use of prenumbered input and output forms. (*Note*: These are used only on important or negotiable documents.)
   The use of prenumbered forms involves the following steps:

- Input documents (such as sales forms) and output documents (such as checks and purchase orders) should be prenumbered when acquired.
- The documents should be contained in a controlled location.
- A simple accounting should be made of the numbers; if any number is missing, it should be investigated.
- Voided documents should be indicated "VOID" and retained to ensure the completeness of the numbering set.

5. Comparative Financial Statements Financial statements produced by the record-keeping system should be comparative; that is, data in the current financial period are compared to data in another,

comparable period. The comparable period might be the previous accounting period, such as last month, or the same month a year ago.
Which is selected will depend on the type of business and on business
fluctuations. Cyclical businesses should compare from year to year,
while businesses with relatively steady business might do better provided with a month-by-month comparison.

In many financial statements it is also important to have *year-to-
date totals*, which show the totality of the current month's balance plus
all the months preceding the current month. When this type of system is
used, the cumulative part is based on either a calendar or a fiscal year,
whichever the business uses.

6. Training   Training is an important control in the use of record-
keeping systems. The objective of training is twofold. First, the people
performing the work need to be trained in the appropriate methods for
documenting and recording financial information. Second, those who
receive financial statements should be trained in how to interpret and
use that information.

Good rules to follow in recording financial information are:

- To confirm the amount recorded with the individual providing the information (such as the customer)
- To verify that any codes used are correct
- To examine the document for reasonableness (for example, ten
  products ordered at $2.98 each should be less than an extended
  amount of $30.00)
- To check any prices or other permanent information for timeliness
  (for example, has there been a recent price increase, and does this
  document reflect that increase?)
- To ensure that all the required information is included
- If it is a computer-produced form, to ensure that financial information
  is right-justified and alphabetic information is left-justified in the field

The type of training that users of financial information need includes:

- Basic accounting
- Reading of financial statements

- Interpretation of financial statements
- Computation and interpretation percentages of, and ratios and relationships between, various financial amounts

WHAT THREATS DO THE KEY CONTROLS ADDRESS?

Control is divided into general and application controls. General controls govern all areas of the business, while application controls are directed specifically at individual business functions such as payroll. Whereas most of the controls discussed earlier in this book have been of the application type, those for record-keeping controls are general controls and thus affect all parts of the business.

The threats to accurate and complete record keeping are also general-type threats. The controls that can be used to address those threats are shown in Figure 11-1. This threat-reduction matrix provides the key to improved record keeping for many businesses.

Key Controls \ Threats	System Too Costly	Data Unreliable	Records Not Used as a Working Tool	Results Not Understood	System Complex to Use
Customized systems and forms	✔	✔	✔	✔	✔
Double-entry bookkeeping		✔			
Multiple use of records	✔				✔
Prenumbered forms		✔			
Comparative financial statements				✔	
Training		✔	✔	✔	

Figure 11-1 RECORD-KEEPING THREAT-REDUCTION MATRIX

IF I CAN ONLY AFFORD TWO CONTROLS, WHAT SHOULD THEY BE?

Good record keeping provides the basis for good business controls. Many of the weaknesses inherent in small businesses can be compensated for by recording and analyzing good financial information. The recommended two controls to make this happen are:

1. *Customized systems and forms.* The record-keeping system must be customized for the needs of the business. If it is not, the type of information needed might not be available, while the information collected may be of only minimal use. Normally it is best for management and the accounting firm to establish jointly the record-keeping system for the organization. This involves not only setting up the records, but deciding whether the system should be automated and what type of financial statements should be produced by the system.

2. *Multiple use of records.* This control minimizes the amount of effort expended on record keeping and maximizes the probability of getting data recorded correctly. The concept requires analyzing what's needed and then determining the easiest way of recording the needed data.

HOW DO I KNOW THE CONTROLS WORK?

Everybody is an expert on record keeping. If you don't believe that, give someone a form or record-keeping process and ask how it might be improved. The person will tell you. In the United States alone there are well over 100,000 different payroll systems. This means that businesses have found at least 100,000 different ways to maintain payroll records. Who says that everyone is not an expert in record keeping?

Management must recognize that there are probably more bad record-keeping systems than there are good ones. The attributes of a good record-keeping system are incorporated into the KISS concept, which means "keep it simple, stupid." The types of tests that should be conducted by management are simplicity tests and integrity tests. The first set of tests ensures that the process is easy to use and the second ensures that the data produced by the system are reliable.

Substantive Tests

These tests are directed at the reliability and integrity of record-keeping systems and include:

- *Number-of-forms test.* If there are more forms than there are employees, the business has too many records. The different forms or documents that an employee uses in his/her work should be totalled to determine how many different forms each employee must understand. The objective of a record-keeping system should be to make record keeping as simple as possible. Consider eliminating forms wherever possible.
- *Record-keeping inaccuracies.* Records should be maintained on the type and frequency of errors occurring in the record-keeping system. These records should be informal but maintained regularly. For a simple format, a yellow pad can be used to write down errors as they occur. Periodically, perhaps quarterly or semiannually, these errors can be categorized. Whenever a high frequency of errors occurs in a single part of a record-keeping system, it is usually indicative of a record-keeping problem and not of a people problem.
- *"Oh, by the way" requests.* These are requests for additional information. They may be made by the company's accountant, by members of management, or by outside agents for tax and other federal, state, and local reporting purposes. If the record-keeping system cannot produce the desired information for running the business, the system should be extended to collect and produce the needed information.

Substantive Test Inconsistencies

This book has proposed a large number of substantive tests to show inconsistencies or inaccuracies in the methods and systems incorporated by the business. The inaccuracies uncovered through these other substantive tests normally mean not only that there are problems in the specific area but also that the record-keeping system is inadequate. Any time the substantive tests show business problems, the solution may be improved record-keeping systems. However, caution should be exercised in increasing the record-keeping system for insignificant or one-of-a-kind problems. A common mistake when a problem occurs is to add new controls and extend record keeping, when in fact that problem may never occur again. Sometimes the solution costs more than the loss associated with the problem.

Internal Control Self-Assessment Checklist

As previously mentioned, record-keeping controls are general controls. This means that the controls as used by management are directed at the entire business. Checklist 8 is designed to assess the adequacy of the general or managerial controls over record keeping. *Yes* answers are indicative of good control practices, while *no* answers may represent a potential control vulnerability. *No* answers should be investigated to determine whether or not the controls need to be strengthened.

CONTROL RULE OF THUMB 28
Don't criticize the advice of your accountant on controls— remember who hired the accountant!

Checklist 8   RECORD-KEEPING SELF-ASSESSMENT

		Response			
Item		Yes	No	N/A	Comments
1. Have a suitable chart of accounts and standard journal entries been developed?					
2. Have guidelines been established for determining the appropriate account distribution on purchased items?					
3. Are schedules prepared for payments so that discounts can be taken?					
4. Are schedules prepared for tax filing and payments in order to avoid overdue and late assessments?					

Checklist 8 RECORD-KEEPING SELF-ASSESSMENT

		Response		
Item	*Yes*	*No*	*N/A*	*Comments*
5. Are agreements, key contracts, stock, and other negotiable and valuable instruments stored in a location with appropriate physical safeguards (safes, safe deposit boxes, and so forth)?				
6. Are financial statements prepared or reviewed by an independent public accountant?				
7. Are the detailed ledger accounts (such as accounts receivable and accounts payable) periodically reconciled to the control totals?				
8. Are accounting records retained in accordance with legal and regulatory requirements? (For example, the IRS requires accounting records to be maintained three full calendar years past the year in question.)				
9. Is the business's public accountant asked to comment annually on the adequacy of the system of record keeping and internal controls? (This is frequently referred to as a *management report.*)				
10. Is double-entry bookkeeping used?				
11. Is office automation used where appropriate?				
12. Is the sales tax properly accounted for?				
13. Is merchandise on loan or consignment properly recorded?				
14. Are financial statements prepared on a timely basis?				
15. Are financial statements prepared frequently enough to assist in business planning?				

Checklist 8   RECORD-KEEPING SELF-ASSESSMENT (Continued)

Item		Response			
		Yes	No	N/A	Comments
16. Do the financial statements show period-to-period comparisons?					
17. Do computer system controls contain the same level of safeguards present in the manual systems that have been automated?					

III
Do the controls work?

Reliance on controls must be based on a knowledge of controls that are in place and effective. This
knowledge comes from performing periodic independent assessments of the adequacy of the system of
internal controls.

12

evaluating the effectiveness, economy, and efficiency of controls

This book is about profitability and control. A business practice that can improve profitability is for management to periodically step back and evaluate its business. An integral part of that review is the assessment of the adequacy of the system of controls. This chapter addresses the review of controls.

Publicly listed corporations, specifically those covered by the Securities Exchange Act of 1934, must have their controls reviewed by a certified public accountant (CPA). Nonpublic corporations may also be required to have this independent assessment in order to acquire bank loans. Regardless of the reason, it is good practice to evaluate the controls periodically, particularly from a profitability perspective.

This chapter describes a step-by-step process on how to conduct a management controls review. The recommended review process builds on the control assessment segments of Chapters 4 through 11 and utilizes the approaches of an auditor and a manager. Both approaches are important in identifying areas in which improvement could increase profitability.

THE NEED FOR CONTROL REVIEW

There are three primary reasons a business would want a controls review:

1. Control reviews are required. Certified public accountants are required for certain corporations in which they express an opinion on

187

the financial statements to publicly report any material weaknesses in the system of internal accounting control. (Internal accounting control is a subset of internal control and relates to the processing and recording of financial transac-tions.) Even if a review is not required, the CPA may be asked, for a variety of reasons including bank loans, to comment on the adequacy of the business's system of controls.

2. The Securities and Exchange Commission has stated that public companies should "review their accounting procedures, systems of internal accounting controls and business practices" in order to take any actions necessary to comply with the requirements of the Foreign Corrupt Practices Act of 1977. Among other things, the act requires public companies to "make and keep books, records, and accounts, which, in reasonable detail, accurately and fairly reflect the transactions and dispositions of the assets of the issuer" and to:

> . . . devise and maintain a system of internal accounting controls sufficient to provide reasonable assurance that—
> i) transactions are executed in accordance with management's general or specific authorization;
> ii) transactions are recorded as necessary (I) to permit preparation of financial statements in conformity with generally accepted accounting principles or any other criteria applicable to such statements, and (II) to maintain accountability for assets;
> iii) access to assets is permitted only in accordance with management's general or specific authorization; and
> iv) the recorded accountability for assets is compared with the existing assets at reasonable intervals and appropriate action is taken with respect to any differences.

3. Inadequate controls can result in vulnerabilities that can contribute directly or indirectly to business losses. Dollars saved through improved controls contribute directly to the profitability of the business.

Companies being audited by CPAs are normally asked to provide the accountant with a written statement about the control practices and problems associated with weaknesses in the control system. The accountant is normally expected to obtain management's written representations on:

1. "Acknowledging management's responsibility for establishing and maintaining the system of internal accounting control

2. Stating that management has disclosed to the accountant all material weaknesses in the system of which they are aware, including those for which believes the cost of corrective action may exceed the benefits

3. Describing any irregularities involving management or employees who have significant roles in the system of internal accounting control

4. Stating whether there were any changes subsequent to the date being reported on that would significantly affect the system of internal accounting control, including any corrective action taken by management with regard to material weaknesses"[1]

For any or all of these reasons, it behooves management to be knowledgeable about the adequacy of its system of internal control. While much of this is done on a day-to-day basis, it is important to conduct a review independent of the day-to-day activities. The objective of this review is, first, to determine the adequacy of controls, and second, to evaluate the impact of any control weaknesses.

CONTROL RULE OF THUMB 29
Problems may never be located if nobody looks for them.

WHAT'S IT LIKE TO BE AN AUDITOR?

One of the duties of auditors is to assess the adequacy of internal control. When management conducts a control review, it will be performing a function closely associated with auditors. This means managers will be asking questions, examining transactions, and so forth. In doing so they may generate "auditor's disease" in their employees.

Auditor's disease means employees getting nervous about what the auditor is doing and why the auditor is doing it. The prospect of an audit by an Internal Revenue Service agent drives fear into the hearts of

---

[1]Statement on Auditing Standards No. 30, American Institute of Certified Public Accountants, July 1980. page 12

many otherwise strong individuals. There is something about the words *audit* and *auditor* that causes even honest people to tremble.

In some audits auditor's disease is a plus factor. For example, the Internal Revenue Service relies on it to keep people honest and in many instances it works. In fact, some people will overpay their taxes rather than face the possibility of an audit. In other situations auditor's disease can be detrimental to the objective of the review. That is true in the case of the management review.

There is no easy cure for auditor's disease. However, the symptoms can be lessened by giving one dose of the following to the employees whose records and activities will be involved in the review:

1. Hold a brief meeting with all the employees involved. The objective of this meeting is to explain to the employees that:

   • Control is essential to the profitability of the business.
   • Control needs to be adjusted periodically.
   • The objective of a management controls review is to determine if such control adjustments are necessary.
   • Employees' input and assistance is needed during the review.
   • The outcome of the review will be to adjust those controls that require adjusting.

2. During the review, explain the process. As you look at the records of individual employees, explain why you want those records, what you are going to do with them, and again solicit the employees' help in identifying potential control vulnerabilities, as well as overcontrolled situations.

CONTROL REVIEW PROCESS

The control review is a judgmental process. It is similar in concept to that of hiring someone for a position in the business. Good guidelines can be given, but the final decision on whether to hire the person is a judgmental decision. The same is true in control assessment. Guidelines can be given, but the final assessment on whether control is adequate is a judgmental decision.

Chapters 1 through 3 in this book were designed to provide sufficient background material to make a reasonable assessment. While management is not expected to be control experts, it is responsible for control. Therefore, it is not unreasonable to assign someone in management the task of assessing controls.

The control assessment is a five-step process, as follows:

Step 1—Identify business threats.

Step 2—Evaluate the internal control environment.

Step 3—Evaluate the key application controls.

Step 4—Assess the adequacy of controls (to reduce the identified threats).

Step 5—Take the necessary corrective action.

CONTROL RULE OF THUMB 30
If you want to be sure controls work correctly, take the time to evaluate them.

Step1 — Identify Business Threats

The purpose of the control review, and of control itself, is to ensure that the business threats are properly reduced. However, there is no purpose in designing and implementing controls unless one or more significant threats have been identified. Therefore, the first step in any control assessment is to identify why controls might be needed.

Chapters 4 through 11 have identified forty-four general business threats. During step 1, each of those threats should be reviewed to determine if it poses a significant risk to the business. Only those threats that are of concern to management should be included in the control assessment process.

The Control Evaluation Worksheet (Figure 12-1) is provided as a tool in conducting your control assessment. This worksheet lists the forty-four business threats described in this book. If there are additional threats of concern to management, add these also to this worksheet.

For each threat that is a concern to management you should indicate the area or supervisor in the business responsible for this specific

Figure 12-1 CONTROL EVALUATION WORKSHEET

Number	Threat to Business	Discussed in Chapter	Area/ Supervisor	Control Environment						Key Application Controls				Evaluation Score
				Organizational Structure	Personnel	Delegation and Communication	Budgets and Financial Reports	Organizational Checks and Balances	EDP Considerations	1	2	3	4	
1	Product shipped or delivered but not billed	4												
2	Wrong product shipped	4												
3	Wrong price calculation	4												
4	Billed to wrong customer	4												
5	Wrong cash collection	4												
6	Cash missing	4												
7	Wrong products stocked	4												
8	Customer will not pay for charge sales	5												

9	Collections will not be timely	5
10	Accounts will be lost	5
11	Receipts will be lost	5
12	Sales will be lost due to tight credit policy	5
13	Paying for product not received	6
14	Paying twice for product	6
15	Purchasing unauthorized product	6
16	Failing to take advantage of discounts, price breaks, or discount periods	6
17	Purchasing too much or unneeded products	6
18	Inventory damaged	7
19	Inventory missing	7

Figure 12-1 CONTROL EVALUATION WORKSHEET (Continued)

Number	Threat to Business	Discussed in Chapter	Area/Supervisor	Control Environment — Organizational Structure	Personnel	Delegation and Communication	Budgets and Financial Reports	Organizational Checks and Balances	EDP Considerations	Key Application Controls 1	2	3	4	Evaluation Score
20	Inventory theft	7												
21	Out-of-stock condition	7												
22	Inventory improperly identified	7												
23	Inventory overvalued	7												
24	Inadequate cash flow	8												
25	Loss of interest	8												
26	Loss of cash	8												
27	Inadequate accounting	8												
28	Incorrect salary payments	9												
29	Statutory sanctions	9												

30	Ineffective use of employees	9
31	Fraud and theft	9
32	Loss of customers or trade secrets	9
33	Employee errors and omissions	9
34	Loss of skilled employees	9
35	Products incorrectly priced	10
36	Inadequate cash	10
37	Inappropriate management decisions	10
38	Failure to benefit from automation	10
39	Company improperly organized	10
40	System too costly	11
41	Data unreliable	11
42	Records not used as a working tool	11
43	Results not understood	11
44	System complex to use	11

threat. If management is unfamiliar with some of the controls or of the magnitude of the threats, the individual listed under "Area/Supervisor" is the one who should be consulted. In addition, if corrective action needs to be taken, this is the individual who most likely will be responsible for taking that action.

Step 2 – Evaluate the Internal Control Environment[2]

The internal control environment established by management has a significant impact on the selection and effectiveness of a company's control procedures and techniques.

The control environment is shaped by several factors. Some are clearly visible, such as a formal corporate-conduct policy statement. Some are intangible, like the competence and integrity of personnel. Some factors, like organizational structure and the way in which management communicates, enforces, and reinforces policy, vary so widely among companies that they can be contrasted more easily than compared. Although it is difficult to measure the significance of each factor, it is generally possible to make an overall evaluation of a company's internal control environment, which is a necessary prelude to the evaluation of control procedures and techniques.

A poor control environment will make some accounting controls inoperative for all intents and purposes. For example, individuals hesitate to challenge a management override of a specific control procedure. On the other hand, a strong control environment, one with tight budgetary controls for example, can have an important bearing on the selection and effectiveness of specific accounting control procedures and techniques.

It is possible for control procedures and techniques to be working in a company with a poor control environment. However, it is unlikely for management to have reasonable assurance that the broad objectives of internal control are being met unless the company has an environment that establishes an appropriate level of control consciousness.

The control environment involves all the employees of a com-

---

[2] This material in step 2 is based on the work performed by the Special Advisory Committee on Internal Accounting Control (report issued by the American Institute of Certified Public Accountants, 1211 Avenue of the Americas, New York, NY 10036, during 1979).

pany. However, the role of management in establishing an appropriate control environment cannot be overemphasized. Leadership in formulating and communicating an appropriate atmosphere of control consciousness must come from the top. That leadership involves creating an appropriate organizational structure, using sound management practices, establishing accountability for performance, and requiring adherence to appropriate standards for ethical behavior, including compliance with applicable laws and regulations. Many companies have found it necessary to formalize such guidance through written policies and procedures. Such formalization is conducive to an environment in which internal controls are likely to be understood and to operate effectively.

The remainder of this section discusses some of the more significant factors that shape the internal control environment.

Organizational Structure   The organizational structure of a company provides the overall framework for the planning, direction, and control of its operations. In general, it involves reporting relationships; functions to be performed by organizational units; and the authority, responsibilities, and constraints of key positions.

The effectiveness of a company's organizational structure depends on how well it serves as a framework for the direction and control of company activities. An effective structure gives appropriate consideration to the following items:

- *Item* How competent are the personnel?
  Discussion Competence of personnel to discharge the responsibilities assigned is important together with a system of measurement of and accountability for performance.
- *Item* Has responsibility been adequately delegated?
  Discussion Delegation of responsibility and authority to deal with matters such as goals and objectives, operating functions, organizational form, management style, regulatory requirements, and financial reporting standards is necessary to ensure functions are adequately performed.
- *Item* Are reports adequate to monitor the performance of people?
  Discussion Budgets and financial reports are needed to monitor the discharge of assigned responsibilities and to monitor the activities at each level in the organizational structure.

- *Item* Have adequate organizational checks and balances been established?
  Discussion It is important to establish checks and balances that separate incompatible activities to preclude absolute control by any single individual or unit, that provide for supervision by higher levels of management, and that provide for monitoring of overall company activities.

The more responsive a company's organizational structure is to its external and internal requirements, the more likely it is to strengthen the accounting control procedures in place. For example, when responsibility is assigned for marketing and production activities but not for inventory management, there may be less control consciousness than when all three are addressed. An effective organizational structure should minimize gaps and overlaps in responsibility assignment.

The larger a company and the more complex its operations, the more desirable it is to document the organizational structure. Organization charts, position descriptions, policy statements, and similar documents are frequently used for that purpose.

Personnel The internal control environment and the control procedures themselves are highly dependent on the competence and integrity of the company's personnel. Professional auditing literature states that "reasonable assurance that the objectives of control are met depends on the competence and integrity of personnel, the independence of their assigned functions, and their understanding of the prescribed procedures."[1]

Those factors are particularly important to maintaining an appropriate internal control environment. Dishonest or incompetent employees can make most control procedures inoperative. For example, misunderstanding of instructions, mistakes of judgment, carelessness, or other personal factors related to competence and integrity can result in errors in the performance of control procedures. Collusion between employees can circumvent certain control procedures. Similarly, management personnel may often be in a position to circumvent or override control procedures intentionally. Accordingly, management

[1]Report of the Special Advisory Committee on Internal Accounting Control, AICPA, September 1978 page 10.

should consider whether the company's policies and procedures with respect to hiring, evaluation, compensation, promotion, training, and so forth are conducive to the employment of competent, honest personnel.

Delegation and Communication of Responsibility and Authority Management should delegate or limit authority in a manner that provides assurance that its responsibilities are effectively discharged. Thus authority for specific matters should be assigned and limited in a manner that permits an effective review of decisions made. For example, the board of directors may choose to retain direct authority to approve or disapprove long-term loan agreements of all types but may decide to delegate the authority to approve or disapprove capital expenditures within established limits. To obtain reasonable assurance that the delegated authority is being exercised appropriately, the board might use such measures as reports (such as financial statements), observation, discussion, and consultation, as well as rely on the organizational structure itself. Each level of management should operate in a similar fashion, delegating authority within reasonable limits while retaining final responsibility. This results in a network of personnel who are specifically authorized to approve or disapprove designated transactions and who are prohibited from engaging in or approving other specified transactions.

At each level in the organization there is a need for a clear understanding of the authority and responsibilities delegated and the relationships individuals have with respect to others in the organization. There is also a need to know the policies, procedures, and activities that directly and indirectly affect individual responsibilities. Appropriate communication is therefore essential to control consciousness. Communication about the delegation of responsibility and authority and about related policies and procedures should be explicit to be effective. To be explicit, communication need not be written, although that may be helpful. The critical test is that those who need to be informed are, in fact, properly informed.

Budgets and Financial Reports The formulation and communication of company goals and objectives enables managers to propose courses of action, receive approval and direction, know what is expected of them, and perform in a complementary, unified manner.

Budgets and financial reports are tools used in that process. When approved, budgets and longer-range plans constitute a form of general authorization. Although the specifics set forth in such budgets and plans will vary with the company's specific circumstances, they should:

• Present for each level of management all material aspects of planned operations for which it has either direct or oversight responsibilities
• Be segmented in a manner that reflects the assigned responsibilities set forth in the plan of organization
• Be updated to reflect management's decisions relative to changes in conditions and circumstances

Financial reports that compare budgeted and actual results and analyze variances, along with the managerial action that results from that analysis, may enable management to identify areas where controls may need to be strengthened. They also provide a means for evaluating performance, help give reasonable assurance that transactions are being executed in accordance with management's authorization, and help develop an attitude of accountability at all levels of the company.

Appropriate reports are a key form of control over the exercise of authority that has been delegated to others. Accordingly, reports assume increased significance at higher levels in the company, to management whose involvement in day-to-day transactions tends to lessen significantly.

Organizational Checks and Balances   The concept of checks and balances is inherent in all aspects of the internal control environment—organizational structure, delegation and communication of responsibility and authority, and budgets and financial reports.

In evaluating checks and balances in an organization, particular attention should be given to the financial control. The activities of the financial control function might be performed by a combination of organizational segments, for example, controllership, treasury, planning, and information systems. Such activities will also involve arrays of reporting relationships that differ depending on the company's organizational structure. The specifics of an effective organizational structure must permit the corporate-level executive(s) responsible for the financial control function to discharge their responsibilities to the chief executive and to the board.

The financial control function is by its nature concerned with the establishment and continuous supervision of the control environment. Activities for which this function should be responsible include the following:

- Design of control procedures and techniques applicable to specific transactions.
- Oversight of specific transactions to assure that they are properly recorded and otherwise satisfy control criteria.
- Design of financial planning and reporting systems that capture the results of actual performance of the organization.
- Issuance of reports that appropriately present both planned and actual financial performance.
- Identification and communication of significant variances from management's plan.

EDP Considerations   The method of electronic data processing (EDP) used by a company may influence its organizational structure and the procedures and techniques used to accomplish the broad objectives of internal accounting control. Accordingly, EDP considerations play an important role in evaluating a company's control environment and procedures.

Because of the characteristics of computer systems and computerized controls, management needs to understand the vulnerabilities and controls for specific business applications and cycles and to understand the controls in the computer processes themselves. The degree of reliance that can be placed on controls exercised by the computer system depends on the degree of control exercised by management over the development and maintenance of the computer system.

Some of the important characteristics of contemporary computer systems are physical concentration of data, concentration of different functions within the EDP activity, and multiple users of common data. Therefore, special consideration should be given to three major threats in an EDP environment:

1. the loss of important information through disaster
2. the ability of a single individual to make unauthorized changes that negate internal accounting controls or permit improper access to assets

3. unintentional loss of assets (for example, through pricing errors on sales invoices because of errors in the master price file)

Some of the tasks frequently performed in the EDP process itself are:

- Initiation, authorization, execution, and reporting of transactions according to preestablished rules. Examples might include interest and depreciation calculations; orders to purchase or ship merchandise; and automatic preparation of checks for repetitive payments, such as dividends, employee benefits, or freight settlements.
- Preparation or processing of documents that authorize the use or disposition of assets. This indirect access may occur in connection with computer-initiated transactions.
- Performance of the full range of accounting functions, that is, recording and classifying, summarizing, and reporting transactions.
- Implementation of accounting controls. Those controls may relate to internally generated transactions, internal processing, or internal files, as well as to data submitted for processing.

The wide range of tasks that may be performed by the EDP process emphasizes the importance of proper methods for developing systems and of management participating in the development process.

Management should also recognize that computer programs are frequently subject to change. If the change process (or program maintenance) is not controlled, an individual can make unauthorized or incorrect changes that can affect the data files unpredictably. For example, internal transactions may be generated; assets may be indirectly accessed by individuals responsible for accounting for the assets; editing and reporting of errors or exceptions may be subverted. Similarly, to the extent that supervisory programs are changed and the change process itself is not controlled, unauthorized transactions may be initiated and the reporting of them suppressed. Finally, to the extent that direct unauthorized access to the computer can occur, data programs can be accidentally or intentionally modified or destroyed.

In considering its organizational structure, management should recognize that the development of contemporary systems consists of identifying the company's business requirements from diverse sources and users and translating the requirements into operational computer instructions. This requires a substantially higher level of coordination among groups within the organization and among technical disciplines than was previously required when systems simply supported individual departments.

Assessing the Strength of the Control Environment   Six control environment areas have been discussed. Each of these will have an impact on the strength of the control environment, with the possible exception of EDP if the information processing of the business has not been automated.

For each threat that is a concern, management should evaluate the adequacy of the six control environmental areas. For example, threat 27 (see Figure 12-1) is that "inadequate accounting" procedures will result in inaccurate, incomplete, or untimely financial data. For this threat, management must decide whether each of the six control environmental areas is such that the controls over inadequate accounting are *fully adequate, adequate,* or *less than adequate.*

The "control environment" columns of Figure 12-1 should be filled out as follows:

Control Assessment	Meaning of Control Assessment	Description
3	Fully adequate	• This category is applied to the control environment areas in which there is little opportunity for a business problem to occur, other than the normal routine problems that are minor in scope.
2	Adequate	• Some control problems and losses could occur in this area and not be prevented or detected by the system of controls in the normal course of doing business.

Score Range	Evaluation	
1	Less than adequate	• The potential for serious problems exists in this area due to weaknesses in the control environment area.

If management felt that the organizational structure, for example, was adequate in addressing the "inadequate accounting" threat, then you should put a "2" in the "organizational structure" column. in order to indicate you believe this area to be adequate.

Step 3 – Evaluate the Key Application Controls

The adequacy of control is determined by both the environmental and the application controls. However, in smaller businesses the environmental controls are normally the stronger of the two and should be relied on more than the application controls.

Chapters 4 through 9 have identified the key application controls in most businesses, while Chapters 10 and 11 have identified additional environmental controls. Many of the environmental controls in Chapters 10 and 11 have already been addressed in the six control environment areas. However, if these additional controls appear to be particularly valuable, they should also be considered in the application categories described in this step of the control assessment process.

For each threat, management should identify the key application controls that management believes are effective for reducing the identified threat. Referring back to the appropriate chapter will help identify the key controls. The assessment process is as follows:

1. Identify up to four key controls that are effective in reducing a threat. (If there are over four, there is probably some redundancy and overlap so that more than four would not add to the adequacy of application controls.) If there are over four key controls in place, pick what you believe are the best four.
2. Using the same assessment method described in step 2, determine the adequacy of each of the selected key application controls. Indicate the assessment on Figure 12-1 using the ratings 1, 2, or 3.
3. On a separate worksheet list the four specific application controls

evaluated and then cross-reference them to the application control columns labeled 1 through 4 on Figure 12-1. (The numbers 1 through 4 are only reference numbers, due to the fact that there are many application controls.)

Step 4 – Assess the Adequacy of Controls

An evaluation score should be prepared for each threat. This evaluation score is used to provide an indicator of the adequacy of control. It requires interpretation. The user of this method is cautioned not to place complete reliance on this number but rather to use it as an indicator in determining the magnitude of each threat.

The evaluation score is calculated as follows:

1. Add up the assessment numbers for all of the key application controls and environmental areas evaluated. (*Note*: There should be an evaluation score for each of the six control evaluation areas but there may be anywhere from four to only one application control column filled in.)

2. Divide that number by the appropriate divisor. Select the divisor according to how many key application controls were evaluated.

Number of Application Controls Evaluated	Divisor
1	7
2	8
3	9
4	10

3. Round the number to the nearest tenth of a digit and put the result in the "evaluation score" column in Figure 12-1.

The suggested interpretation of the evaluation score is as follows:

Score Range	Evaluation
1.0-1.4	This is a serious threat to the business and requires strengthening of controls.

(*cont.*)

Score Range	Evaluation
1.5-1.8	This threat represents a vulnerability to the business. Unless one or two of the control areas are exceptionally strong, control action should be taken to further reduce this business threat.
1.9-2.2	This area appears reasonably well controlled. There are probably potential problems, but unless experience has shown them to be of significant scope, the controls do not need adjusting.
2.3-2.5	This threat is very well controlled. It should not be of any concern to management.
2.6-3.0	The probability exists that this threat is overcontrolled. Unless these controls are also applicable to other threats, management may want to consider eliminating the controls that are costly to conduct.

Any of the threats in the categories suggesting improvement of controls should be listed. Management should then apply judgment to determine whether these threats pose a significant risk to the business. If so, they should be listed as potential vulnerabilities to the business.

Step 5 – Take the Necessary Corrective Action

The vulnerabilities identified in step 4 should be ranked according to magnitude of threat to the business. Management should address the higher-ranked threats first and the lower-ranked threats as time becomes available.

The chapters in which each of the threats is discussed provide immediately implementable solutions to those threats. Management should refer to the appropriate chapter and select those controls designed to reduce the threat of concern. It is generally good practice to conduct a second assessment a few weeks or months after the controls have been strengthened.

Control Evaluation Example

Let's briefly walk through an example of how management might evaluate one of the forty-four threats. Figure 12-2 is a completed control evaluation worksheet for threat 1, "product shipped or delivered but not billed." Note that more explanation of the meaning of this threat is discussed in Chapter 4. Let us further assume that the individual in our business in charge of shipping product is Bill Smith. We are now ready to complete the five-step evaluation process for the threat that products shipped will not be billed to our customers.

Step 1—Identify Business Threats   We will assume the business in question ships inventory and thus the threat is a real threat for the business. Therefore, the process continues and we proceed to step 2.

Step 2—Evaluate the Internal Control Environment   Each one of the six internal control environments must be evaluated for this specific threat. It might be done as follows:

- *Organization structure.* Bill Smith is in charge of the shipping area, which is separated from the billing area. Therefore, we could assume that the organization structure was fully adequate.
- *Personnel.* Bill Smith is a good employee but lacks some of the accounting and mathematical skills that might be desirable. Therefore, we would rate personnel adequate.
- *Delegation and communication.* Bill Smith has most of the authority he needs, and management does communicate with him periodically. Perhaps it could be better, but delegation and communication still can be rated adequate.
- *Budgets and financial reports.* There is no budgeting or financial report relating to inventory shortages. Therefore, this environmental control is less than adequate.
- *Organizational checks and balances.* The order for the product is taken by one person, shipped by Bill Smith, and then billed by a third. This appears to be, for a business our size, fully adequate.
- *EDP considerations.* The business has an installed computer system. There are problems in the perpetual inventory records; therefore, this environmental area is rated less than adequate.

Figure 12-2 CONTROL EVALUATION WORKSHEET EXAMPLE

| Number | Threat to Business | Discussed in Chapter | Area/Supervisor | Control Environment | | | | | | Key Application Controls | | | | Evaluation Score |
				Organizational Structure	Personnel	Delegation and Communication	Budgets and Financial Reports	Organizational Checks and Balances	EDP Considerations	1 Formal and Timely Documentation of Sales	2 Customer Confirmation Copy	3 Authorization Needed to Move Product	4	
1	Product shipped or delivered but not billed	4	Bill Smith	3	2	2	1	3	1	2	2	3		2.1

Using the numerical ratings for adequacy, we fill in the "control environment" columns on Figure 12-2.

Step 3—Evaluate the Key Application Controls   There are three key controls relating to this threat, which are (see Chapter 4 for an explanation of these controls):

1. Formal and timely documentation of sales
2. Customer confirmation copy
3. Authorization needed to move product

The first two controls are assessed as adequate and are rated "2," while the third is strictly enforced and therefore rated "3," fully adequate. Based on the order in which the controls are listed above, we call these controls key applications 1, 2, and 3 and fill in the ratings on Figure 12-2.

Step 4—Assess the Adequacy of Controls   The numerical evaluation scores total 19. Since there are three key controls, the total score of 19 is divided by 9, producing an evaluation score of 2.1.

Going to the evaluation table given in the section describing step 4, we see that the 2.1 score is evaluated as: "This area appears reasonably well controlled. There are probably potential problems, but unless experience has shown them to be of significant scope, the controls do not need adjusting."

Step 5—Take the Necessary Corrective Action   In this example, it does not appear that corrective action is needed immediately. However, if there are other more severe problems, they should be addressed by management. Be cautioned that this whole control evaluation indicator is just that—an indicator. Management should still use judgment and intuition in making the assessment.

MONITORING COMPLIANCE TO CONTROLS

Management should monitor compliance with established control procedures to obtain reasonable assurance that the controls in place continue to be appropriate to the threat and that they continue to function properly. *Monitoring* takes place through management supervision, representations, audits, compliance tests, approval and control of changes to procedures, and so forth. Monitoring is an integral part of the continuing process of evaluating the control environment and the effectiveness of control procedures.

CONTROL RULE OF THUMB 31

Being right half the time beats being half right all the time.

13

who controls the controls? — the big picture

There is a time and a place for everything. There is a time to control, and a time not to control. Management must know when to do which and how to tell employees the difference between a situation requiring control and a situation in which they can bypass controls. For example, if the control policy says that returns are only made when accompanied by a sales slip and one of your best customers walks in to return a product without a sales slip—that's the time to relax controls.

This chapter is about the day-to-day, practical aspects of control. It is in part a sermon, in part a recounting of experiences learned through painful control encounters, and part some suggestions on how to make people "like" controls. Hopefully, this chapter will answer the questions that may have bothered you while reading the rest of the book.

This chapter has a beginning, a middle, and an end. The beginning attempts to define the practical aspects of management control responsibilities. The middle of the chapter is a question-and-answer section on necessary questions about control not covered earlier in the book. The end of the chapter is a pep talk to encourage you to do what you know you should do about implementing and enforcing control in your business.

MANAGEMENT'S "REAL" CONTROL RESPONSIBILITIES

The real responsibility of senior management of the business is to be a total believer in control. It is not enough to write control procedures, to ask people to follow control procedures, or to put up posters and slogans encouraging people to "do it the company way." What is needed is for management to be a believer, a leader, and an exemplar of someone following and enforcing control.

Good control leadership only occurs from personal example. A manager cannot tell the staff to refrain from using the petty cash for personal purposes and then periodically "borrow" money from the fund for lunch or other questionable uses. Management must remain above reproach in control dealings, expect others to do the same, and discipline those who do not.

The real responsibilities of management for creating an example and environment in which control will flourish can best be expressed in a series of ten commandments:

1. Clearly establish the objectives of control in the business.
2. View yourself as someone who will follow all the controls perfectly.
3. Do not accept deviations from control for personal reasons.
4. Reprimand employees for every control violation.
5. Make the punishment for control violations consistent with the magnitude of the infraction.
6. Evaluate employees' performance on their attitudes about control.
7. Investigate the impact of any control vulnerability.
8. Design controls such that they do not tempt anyone to steal.
9. Periodically assess the adequacy of controls.
10. Be a believer in control and control principles.

CONTROL Q'S and A'S

A very successful business person once said, "There is more than one way to skin a cat." Obviously, he was referring to control. There are many ways to achieve the same control objective. In discussing control concepts and control methods throughout this book, the following questions were not answered but may have occurred to you as you read the control solutions.

Question: Can I control the amount of tax I pay to the federal, state, and local governments?

Answer: Taxing authorities normally provide a series of options that affect the amount of tax paid. For example, businesses can use accelerated depreciation or straight-line depreciation. Using straight-line, they would pay significantly more tax than if they used the accelerated depreciation method. Early in each tax year management should get together with the tax accountant and do tax planning for the year. It is only through tax planning that taxes can be minimized.

Question: Why would I want to control the amount of profit I make?
Answer: Businesses may want to increase or decrease their profit in any year for a variety of reasons. The primary reason for increasing profits is to obtain bank loans or to sell stock. The primary reason for decreasing profit is to pay less taxes. The most common variables that can be adjusted that affect profit include:

- Method of depreciating assets
- Acquiring or not acquiring additional fixed assets
- Acquiring or not acquiring items that are immediately expensed, such as office supplies
- Declaring or not declaring employee bonuses at year end

Question: What should I do if I suspect one of my employees is stealing from the business?
Answer: Confronting an individual whom you suspect is defrauding your business is very tricky. Two negative things can happen if you do so. First, if you are wrong, the person may enter a countersuit against you for defamation of character. Second, if you don't know what you are doing, you may ruin the case against that individual.
   An individual should never be confronted in a one-on-one situation. It is best to have a third person involved, ideally someone who understands either the law or the investigation. If possible, this should be a lawyer or law enforcement official.

Question: If I suspect someone is stealing from me, what type of evidence should I obtain?
Answer: Only original documents count as evidence. Do not copy records and retain them as evidence. Retain the original rec-

ords. The best evidence is the original source documents prepared or manipulated by the individual suspected of fraud.

Question: If a little control is good, isn't a lot of control better?

Answer: The right amount of control reduces threat to an acceptable
level. More or less control than that is a poor use of business
funds. Too little control wastes money through unnecessary
losses, while too much control wastes money because more is
spent on the control than is received in the benefits from those
controls.

Question: Do I have to balance my financial records to the penny?

Answer: Very few organizations maintain their financial records with
complete accuracy. The argument for balancing to the penny is
that an error may contain multiple other tiny errors. Tracking all
of these down is not an economical approach, so that when the
books can be balanced to within a few dollars, it is usually not
worth continuing to find small errors; spending $100 to look for
a $5 error is generally unwise.

Question: What is the best way to simplify my record-keeping
system?

Answer: The use of automation is the answer to simplicity. The computer is very good at doing repetitive clerical work, while very poor
at doing jobs requiring intuition and judgment. Businesses should
attempt to let machines do what machines do best and let people
do what people do best.

Question: How long must I retain my records for control purposes?

Answer: Most taxing authorities require that tax records be retained
three full calendar years past the year in which the records apply.
The exception to this is that if fraud is suspected. Contracts and
other legal documents should be retained for a seven-year period.
For questions regarding the length of time a financial record
should be retained, ask your accountant; if it is a legal document,
ask your lawyer.

Question: What is an audit trail, and do I need one?

Answer: An *audit trail* enables you to trace transactions from the
original source document to the financial statements of the business, or to identify all of the source documents that comprise a
financial balance. Audit trails are necessary for two primary pur-

poses: first, to substantiate balances for tax purposes; second, to answer questions from customers that require substantiation of how a particular event or transaction occurred.

Question: Must my controls be able to substantiate every penny expended by my business?

Answer: Technically, you should be able to substantiate every penny, but in practice no one, including the Internal Revenue Service, expects you to. The underlying basis of control is that it should not cost more to control an event than the event is worth. If the events being controlled appear reasonable and the amounts are not substantial, controls that can assure accuracy to within plus or minus $25 are normally considered reasonable.

Question: What type of documents should be produced from my business planning process?

Answer: Any business plan should produce the following four documents:

1. Work program
2. Work schedule
3. Budget
4. Cash-flow statement

The work program states what you plan to do; the schedule states when you plan to do it; the budget indicates how much revenue it will generate and how much it will cost; and the cash-flow statement determines whether you have sufficient cash to do it.

Question: If I can afford it, should I have my accountant prepare my work plan and budget and design the controls so that I can accomplish my objectives?

Answer: The plan, budget, and schedule are management's objectives for the business. The accountant can help in this process but cannot do the work. Management must not only develop the plan but must also implement it. Unless sufficiently committed to developing the plan, it is unlikely that management will have the commitment to implement it.

Question: How frequently should I adjust my controls?

Answer: If the threat in question is causing the business to lose a

significant amount of funds, the controls should be adjusted immediately. On the other hand, it is confusing to employees to
make changes too frequently. Therefore, it is better to group control changes and make the series at one time. Doing this every
three months is about all the change most employees can assimi-
late into their daily work.

Question: If I get a computer, will I be able to control it without
knowing how it works?

Answer: Some basic computer skills are of course advisable, but control objectives and principles do not change whether the system is
manual or automated. For example, in a manual system, management would want to know who is accountable for making a sale or
giving a customer a credit. The same information is needed in an
automated system. While there are some new threats that occur
only with computer systems, most of the threats are the ones
described in this book. The same types of controls that are effective
in manual systems are generally effective in all but the very large
automated systems. For a more detailed discussion of computer
systems, read *Survival Guide to Computer Systems*, published by
CBI, (William E. Perry 1982).

Question: What type of controls are placed on my business in regard
to hiring and firing employees?

Answer: Generally, you are free to hire the most qualified individual
for a job and to fire an incompetent employee. However, you are
not allowed to violate Equal Employment Opportunity regulations, such as discriminating against employees because of age,
race, religion, or sex. While the burden of proof is on the
employee with the discrimination complaint, the hiring practices
used by your business will be partially judged by the type of employees you have hired and fired in the past.

Question: How do I really know that my controls are synchronized
with the processing needs of the business?

Answer: Use the "squeak" test. If employees complain or squeak too
much, you can be assured that the controls are hampering their
productivity. On the other hand, if your employees never mention
controls, the controls are probably effective and consistent with the
needs of the business.

Question: Will my employees understand what I am trying to do in building an adequate system of internal control?

Answer: Most employees don't know what a control is. They view a control as something that prohibits them from doing something they would either like to do or think they should be able to do. Most of the controls we have talked about in this book would be viewed as procedures or work methods by the employees.

Question: Should I have my books audited?

Answer: Unless your business has to be audited or a bank requires an audit before making you a loan, it is generally not economical. The procedures outlined in Chapter 12 will permit you to perform an in-house audit. If you approach that assessment process with a dedication for determining the adequacy of controls, your in-house audit will serve business purposes normally as well as would an audit conducted by an independent accountant.

Question: How do I know that my accountant is doing a good job in closing my books or in advising me on the adequacy of my controls?

Answer: Your accountant should be advising you on ways to improve your profitability. If he or she merely closes your books and provides you with financial statements, you are not getting your money's worth. A good rule of thumb is to ask other business colleagues what type of service they are getting from their accountants. If you are not getting equivalent service, it is a good time to change accountants.

Question: If I change a business process, should I change the controls over that process at the same time?

Answer: Yes! Controls have a habit of getting out of synch with the needs of the business. The net result may be that the business may be better off without the control. For example, if the number of checks being cashed by customers increases significantly and the approval procedure centers around the owner of the business, this may delay business to the point where customers get discouraged and shop elsewhere.

Controls should change either as the threats change or as the methods of doing business change. Changes to the threat affect the strength of the control; controls should be either relaxed or tightened according to the change in magnitude of the threat. Changes in the method of doing business require intermeshing the controls with those methods to avoid disrupting the normal business work flow.

CASHING IN ON CONTROL

Control need not be a dirty word but, rather, a means of achieving a stated objective.

Control is the secret to profitability in most companies. When properly used, it is the secret ingredient of success. You have read my story and I have given you the key to the kingdom—control. Use it wisely; you will be rewarded with increased profits.

CONTROL RULE OF THUMB 32
If control is to be, it is up to me.

Appendix

control rules of thumb

CONTROL RULES OF THUMB

Number	Rule	Included in Chapter
1	You can't manage what you can't control.	1
2	When you want to know who is responsible for control, look in a mirror.	1
3	Controls don't earn money—but they can increase profits.	1
4	A good system of internal control keeps honest people honest.	2
5	The way that you spell relief from business crime is I-N-T-E-R-N-A-L C-O-N-T-R-O-L.	2
6	Most large embezzlements begin as petty theft that is allowed to continue without reprimand.	3
7	In any threat situation, management must determine whether it is more economical to accept losses than to control them.	3
8	The fulfillment of management's control responsibility begins with a plan of action. It concludes when that plan of action is in place and working.	3
9	It is generally better to err on the side of too few controls than too many, since it is easier to add controls than to delete them.	4
10	Controls should be established as early as possible in each activity.	4
11	If controls are burdensome and time consuming, they are not effective. Controls should improve the process, not hinder it.	4
12	Many corporations have gone bankrupt due to lax credit policies, but very few have gone under due to tight credit policies.	5
13	Let the nonpaying customers buy from your competitors. This increases your competitors' sales and increases your profitability.	5
14	If no credit purchases become uncollectible, your credit policy is too tight. On the other hand, if too many receivables become uncollectible, your credit policies are too loose.	5
15	Guard your receivables as you would cash in your cash box. They are equally valuable.	5
16	Never feel pleased about the money received for inventory sold as scrap. It doesn't take many brains to sell dollar bills for twenty five cents.	6

CONTROL RULES OF THUMB

Number	Rule	Included in Chapter
17	Managerial scrutiny and instinct are one of the strongest controls for detecting problems in a small business.	6
18	In designing controls, if there is ever a choice between the concerns of incompetence and greed, incompetence should win every time.	7
19	Pay your accountant to set up your company's accounting records. It is money well invested.	8
20	Income earned on the investment of cash is a 100 percent contribution to bottom-line profit.	8
21	No employee should be in a position to both steal and conceal—that is, take cash or inventory and then adjust the books so that the theft would not be uncovered by the accounting system.	8
22	The control should be applied at the point in the system where the threat is the greatest.	8
23	If employee productivity is a problem, the cause of the problem is management.	9
24	It is not true that volume sales on a product will make up for what you lose on an individual sale. The more you sell of a loss leader, the more you will lose.	10
25	Decisions based on fact are right much more often than are decisions based on intuition.	10
26	If you don't have a plan to tell where you are going, you will probably not get there; and if you do, you won't know you've arrived.	10
27	The final test in assessing the adequacy of any part of the business is the amount of profit generated.	10
28	Don't criticize the advice of your accountant on controls--remember who hired the accountant!	11
29	Problems may never be located if nobody looks for them.	12
30	If you want to be sure controls work correctly, take the time to evaluate them.	12
31	Being right half the time beats being half right all the time.	12
32	If control is to be, it is up to me.	13

index

DATE DUE
